Step-by-Step German

From Alphabet to Conversation

Sophia S.

My First Picture Book Inc.

Copyright © 2024 by My First Picture Book Inc.

All rights reserved.

No portion of this book may be reproduced in any form without written permission from the publisher or author, except as permitted by U.S. copyright law.

Contents

1. Introduction to German — 1
2. German Alphabet and Pronunciation — 5
3. Basic Greetings and Introductions — 9
4. Numbers and Counting — 13
5. Days, Months, and Seasons — 18
6. Colors and Shapes — 22
7. Family and Relationships — 26
8. Common Phrases and Expressions — 30
9. Basic Grammar: Nouns and Articles — 34
10. Basic Grammar: Verbs and Tenses — 38
11. Basic Grammar: Adjectives and Adverbs — 43
12. Asking Questions in German — 48
13. Food and Drink Vocabulary — 53
14. Shopping and Money Vocabulary — 58
15. Time and Dates — 63
16. Intermediate Grammar: Cases (Nominative, Accusative) — 68
17. Intermediate Grammar: Cases (Dative, Genitive) — 72
18. Pronouns and Possessives — 76
19. Prepositions and Conjunctions — 81
20. Describing People and Things — 86
21. Travel and Transportation Vocabulary — 91
22. Housing and Accommodation Vocabulary — 96
23. Health and Body Vocabulary — 101

24.	Jobs and Professions	106
25.	Education and School Vocabulary	111
26.	Entertainment and Leisure Activities	116
27.	Sports and Hobbies	121
28.	Nature and Environment	126
29.	Common Idioms and Expressions	131
30.	Making Comparisons	135
31.	Advanced Grammar: Subordinate Clauses	139
32.	Advanced Grammar: Passive Voice	143
33.	Advanced Grammar: Reflexive Verbs	148
34.	Advanced Grammar: Modal Verbs	152
35.	Advanced Vocabulary: Abstract Nouns	157
36.	Formal and Informal Language	162
37.	Cultural Etiquette and Customs	166
38.	Science and Technology Vocabulary	171
39.	Business and Economics Vocabulary	176
40.	Media and Communications Vocabulary	181
41.	Advanced Conversation Topics	186
42.	Translation Techniques	191
43.	Interpreting Techniques	196
44.	German Dialects and Regional Variations	201
45.	Professional Language Use	205
46.	Traveling, Living, and Working in Germany	210
47.	Final Review and Assessment	215

Chapter 1

Introduction to German

Welcome to the World of German!

Learning a new language is like opening a door to a whole new world. In this book, we're going to take you on an exciting journey to discover the German language, which is spoken by over 100 million people around the globe! Imagine being able to greet someone in German, read signs in Germany, or even watch your favorite German cartoons without needing subtitles. Doesn't that sound cool?

Why Learn German?

You might wonder, "Why should I learn German?" Well, here are some fantastic reasons:

- **German is the most widely spoken language in Europe:** That's right! Not only is it spoken in Germany, but also in Austria, Switzerland, and parts of Belgium and Luxembourg.

- **It opens up future opportunities:** Germany is known for its science, technology, and engineering. Knowing German could help you study or work in these fields one day!

- **It connects you with new people:** Imagine making friends with kids your age from different countries who speak German. Language is a bridge that connects people.

- **It's fun and challenging:** Learning German can be like solving a puzzle. You start with small pieces, like words and sounds, and then put them together to form sentences and stories!

What Will We Learn in This Book?

This book is designed especially for you, a young learner who is curious and eager to explore. We will start from the very basics and guide you all the way to becoming confident in speaking, reading, and understanding German. Here's a sneak peek into some of the exciting things we'll learn:

Getting Started with the German Alphabet

We'll begin with the **German alphabet**. Did you know that it's almost the same as the English alphabet, with just a few new letters? You'll learn to pronounce them correctly and understand how they sound in different words. For example, the German letter 'ß' is pronounced like the double 's' in "kiss." This section will be easy to follow and filled with fun examples!

Basic Greetings and Introductions

Once you know the letters, you can start forming words! We'll teach you how to greet someone, say hello, and introduce yourself. In German, "Hello" is "Hallo" (pronounced: hah-loh) and "My name is" is "Mein Name ist" (pronounced: mine nah-meh ist). Imagine being able to introduce yourself in German – how exciting!

Counting and Numbers

Numbers are everywhere – on clocks, in games, and when you count your candies! You'll learn to count in German from 1 to 100 and beyond. For example, the number 1 is "eins" (pronounced: ayns), and the number 10 is "zehn" (pronounced: tsayn). We'll make it easy and fun with games and practice.

Days, Months, and Seasons

Next, we'll learn about the **days of the week**, **months of the year**, and **seasons** in German. Knowing these will help you talk about your birthday, your favorite season, and even plan a trip! For example, "Monday" in German is "Montag" (pronounced: mon-tahg), and "January" is "Januar" (pronounced: yah-noo-ahr).

Colors and Shapes

Colors make everything more beautiful, and in this chapter, you'll learn the names of different colors and shapes in German. Did you know that "red" in German is "rot" (pronounced: roht) and "circle" is "Kreis" (pronounced: kryss)? You'll have fun naming colors and shapes in German!

Talking About Your Family

We'll also learn how to talk about our **family** and the people we love. You'll discover how to say "mother," "father," "brother," and "sister" in German. For example, "mother" is "Mutter" (pronounced: moot-er), and "father" is "Vater" (pronounced: fah-ter). This chapter will help you describe your family to new friends.

Common Phrases and Expressions

You will learn many useful phrases that will help you start simple conversations. For example, you'll learn to say "How are you?" in German: "Wie geht's?" (pronounced: vee gates). These phrases are super handy and will make you sound like a real German speaker!

Basics of German Grammar

Understanding **grammar** is like learning the rules of a game. First, we'll learn about **nouns** (like "cat" or "school") and **articles** (like "the" or "a"). In German, every noun has a special gender (masculine, feminine, or neuter), and this will help us know which article to use.

Next, we'll learn about **verbs** (action words like "run" or "eat") and **tenses** (past, present, future). You'll also learn about **adjectives** (describing words like "big" or "happy") and **adverbs** (words that describe actions, like "quickly" or "carefully"). These are the building blocks to forming sentences in German.

Asking Questions

Questions are important for learning and making friends! You'll learn how to ask simple questions in German like, "What is your name?" or "Where are you from?". For example, "What is your name?" is "Wie heißt du?" (pronounced: vee hysst doo).

Food, Shopping, and Everyday Life

Imagine ordering your favorite ice cream in German or buying a souvenir at a German shop! We'll teach you the names of foods, drinks, and other things you might need when shopping or eating out. You'll also learn words for everyday objects around you.

Talking About Time and Dates

We will explore how to tell time in German and talk about different times of the day, weeks, months, and years. For example, "What time is it?" in German is "Wie spät ist es?" (pronounced: vee shpate ist ess).

Moving to Intermediate and Advanced Levels

Once you master the basics, we'll move to more intermediate topics. You'll learn about **cases** in German (nominative, accusative, dative, and genitive), which help us understand who is doing what in a sentence. You'll also learn about **pronouns**, **possessives**, and **prepositions**.

Finally, we will cover **advanced topics** like **subordinate clauses**, **passive voice**, and even **German dialects**. We'll help you sound like a native speaker with special lessons on **idioms**, **expressions**, and how to use German in different situations like business or formal conversations.

Chapter 2

German Alphabet and Pronunciation

Welcome to the world of the German alphabet! Just like in English, the German language uses the same basic letters, from A to Z. However, there are a few differences in how some of these letters sound and a few special characters that we will learn about. By the end of this chapter, you will know how to say each letter, understand their unique sounds, and start reading simple words in German!

The German Alphabet

The German alphabet has 26 letters, just like the English alphabet. Here they are:

A, B, C, D, E, F, G, H, I, J, K, L, M, N, O, P, Q, R, S, T, U, V, W, X, Y, Z

Now, let's learn how to pronounce each letter. Some letters are pronounced just like in English, while others have unique German sounds. We'll go through each letter and show you how to say them!

Pronouncing the Letters

- **A** (pronounced: ah like in "car")
- **B** (pronounced: beh like "bay")
- **C** (pronounced: tseh, similar to "ts" in "cats")
- **D** (pronounced: deh like "day")
- **E** (pronounced: eh like in "bed")
- **F** (pronounced: eff like in "fun")

- **G** (pronounced: geh like "gay")
- **H** (pronounced: hah like in "hat")
- **I** (pronounced: ee like in "see")
- **J** (pronounced: yot, sounds like "y" in "yellow")
- **K** (pronounced: kah like "car")
- **L** (pronounced: el like in "love")
- **M** (pronounced: em like in "man")
- **N** (pronounced: en like in "no")
- **O** (pronounced: oh like in "go")
- **P** (pronounced: peh like "pay")
- **Q** (pronounced: koo, always paired with "u" like in "queen")
- **R** (pronounced: err, a rolling sound from the back of the throat)
- **S** (pronounced: ess like in "sun")
- **T** (pronounced: teh like "tay")
- **U** (pronounced: oo like in "moon")
- **V** (pronounced: fau, sounds like "f" in "fish")
- **W** (pronounced: veh, sounds like "v" in "van")
- **X** (pronounced: iks like "ks" in "box")
- **Y** (pronounced: ypsilon, like "ü" in "cute")
- **Z** (pronounced: tset, like "ts" in "cats")

Special Characters in German

In addition to these letters, the German alphabet has a few special characters that are important to learn:

- **Ä, Ö, Ü** – These are the German umlaut vowels. The two dots above the letters change their sound. For example, **Ä** is pronounced like "eh" in "bed," **Ö** is like "i" in "bird," and **Ü** is similar to "u" in "huge" but with rounded lips.

- **ß** (called Eszett or "sharp S") – This letter is pronounced like "ss" in "kiss." It is used only in lower case and never at the beginning of a word.

Vowel Sounds

Vowels in German can have both short and long sounds. The sound depends on how the word is spelled. Let's explore the vowels:

- **A**: Short sound like "ah" in "cat"; Long sound like "ah" in "car".

- **E**: Short sound like "e" in "bet"; Long sound like "ay" in "say".

- **I**: Short sound like "i" in "sit"; Long sound like "ee" in "see".

- **O**: Short sound like "o" in "pot"; Long sound like "oh" in "go".

- **U**: Short sound like "u" in "put"; Long sound like "oo" in "moon".

Consonant Sounds

Many German consonants sound like English, but there are a few differences to remember:

- **J**: Pronounced like "y" in "yellow".

- **V**: Pronounced like "f" in "fun".

- **W**: Pronounced like "v" in "van".

- **Z**: Pronounced like "ts" in "cats".

- **R**: A special rolling sound that comes from the back of the throat, almost like a soft growl!

Tips for Pronunciation

When you see a German word, try breaking it down into smaller parts, or syllables. This will make it easier to pronounce. For example, the word "Hallo" (pronounced: hah-loh) can be broken into "Hal" and "lo." Practice saying each syllable slowly, then put them together to say the whole word.

Practicing with Simple Words

Let's practice with some simple German words to get comfortable with these sounds:

- **Mama** (pronounced: mah-mah) – means "Mom".

- **Katze** (pronounced: kaht-tsuh) – means "Cat".

- **Hund** (pronounced: hoont) – means "Dog".

- **Apfel** (pronounced: ahp-fel) – means "Apple".

- **Brot** (pronounced: broht) – means "Bread".

Understanding Stress and Intonation

In German, the first syllable of a word is usually stressed. For example, in the word "**Katze**" (cat), the first syllable "Kat" is stressed, and the "ze" is pronounced more softly. Pay attention to stress patterns to make your pronunciation sound more natural.

Key Points to Remember

- **Alphabet Basics:** Learn the 26 letters of the German alphabet and their pronunciations.

- **Special Characters:** Understand the umlaut vowels (Ä, Ö, Ü) and the Eszett (ß).

- **Vowels and Consonants:** Practice both short and long sounds of vowels and unique consonant sounds.

- **Breaking Down Words:** Break words into syllables to improve pronunciation.

- **Stress Patterns:** Remember to stress the first syllable in most German words.

Chapter 3

Basic Greetings and Introductions

Now that you know the German alphabet, it's time to start speaking! In this chapter, we will learn some basic greetings and how to introduce ourselves in German. These are the first things you say when meeting someone new, so they are very important. By the end of this chapter, you'll be able to say "hello," ask someone how they are, and introduce yourself, all in German!

How to Say "Hello" in German

Let's start with the most common word in any language: "Hello!" In German, there are a few different ways to greet someone, depending on the time of day and how formal you want to be. Here are the most common greetings:

- **Hallo** (pronounced: hah-loh) – This is the most common way to say "hello" in German. It's informal and can be used with friends, family, and people you know well.

- **Guten Morgen** (pronounced: goo-ten mor-gen) – This means "Good morning" and is used until around 10 or 11 a.m.

- **Guten Tag** (pronounced: goo-ten tahk) – This means "Good day" and is used from late morning until early evening. It's a bit more formal than "Hallo."

- **Guten Abend** (pronounced: goo-ten ah-bent) – This means "Good evening" and is used after 5 or 6 p.m.

Asking "How Are You?" in German

After saying hello, it's polite to ask how someone is doing. In German, there are several ways to do this, depending on how formal or informal you want to be:

- **Wie geht's?** (pronounced: vee gates) – This is the informal way of asking "How are you?" It's like asking "How's it going?" in English and can be used with friends, family, and people your age.

- **Wie geht es Ihnen?** (pronounced: vee gate es ee-nen) – This is the formal way of asking "How are you?" Use it with adults you don't know well or in a polite situation.

When someone asks you "Wie geht's?" or "Wie geht es Ihnen?", you can answer:

- **Mir geht es gut** (pronounced: meer gate es goot) – This means "I am doing well."
- **Mir geht es schlecht** (pronounced: meer gate es shlekht) – This means "I am not doing well."
- **Es geht** (pronounced: es gate) – This means "I'm okay" or "It's going."

Introducing Yourself in German

Next, let's learn how to introduce yourself. This is very important when meeting new people. Here are the basic phrases you will need:

- **Ich heiße...** (pronounced: ikh hys-suh) – This means "My name is..." For example, "Ich heiße Anna" means "My name is Anna."
- **Mein Name ist...** (pronounced: mine nah-meh ist) – This is another way to say "My name is..." It's a bit more formal.
- **Ich bin...** (pronounced: ikh bin) – This means "I am..." and is used to tell someone your name, profession, or where you are from. For example, "Ich bin Schüler" means "I am a student."

When you want to ask someone their name, you can say:

- **Wie heißt du?** (pronounced: vee hysst doo) – This is the informal way of asking "What is your name?"
- **Wie heißen Sie?** (pronounced: vee hys-sen zee) – This is the formal way of asking "What is your name?" Use this with adults or in formal situations.

Introducing Others

If you want to introduce a friend or family member to someone, here are some phrases to help you:

- **Das ist...** (pronounced: das ist) – This means "This is..." You can use it to introduce someone. For example, "Das ist mein Freund" means "This is my friend."

- **Er heißt...** (pronounced: air hysst) – This means "His name is..." For example, "Er heißt Max" means "His name is Max."

- **Sie heißt...** (pronounced: zee hysst) – This means "Her name is..." For example, "Sie heißt Julia" means "Her name is Julia."

Polite Words and Phrases

Being polite is very important in any language. Here are some polite words and phrases that will help you in conversations:

- **Bitte** (pronounced: bit-teh) – This means "Please."

- **Danke** (pronounced: dahn-keh) – This means "Thank you."

- **Entschuldigung** (pronounced: ent-shool-dee-goong) – This means "Excuse me" or "I'm sorry."

- **Ja** (pronounced: yah) – This means "Yes."

- **Nein** (pronounced: nine) – This means "No."

Talking About Where You Are From

People often ask where you are from when you meet them. Here's how to say it in German:

- **Ich komme aus...** (pronounced: ikh kom-meh owss) – This means "I come from..." For example, "Ich komme aus den USA" means "I come from the USA."

- **Ich wohne in...** (pronounced: ikh voh-neh in) – This means "I live in..." For example, "Ich wohne in Berlin" means "I live in Berlin."

Basic Farewells in German

Just like in English, there are many ways to say goodbye in German. Here are the most common ones:

- **Tschüss** (pronounced: chooss) – This is an informal way to say "Bye." It's used with friends and family.

- **Auf Wiedersehen** (pronounced: owf vee-der-zay-en) – This is a formal way to say

"Goodbye." It literally means "Until we see each other again."

- **Bis bald** (pronounced: bis bahlt) – This means "See you soon."

- **Gute Nacht** (pronounced: goo-teh nahkht) – This means "Good night."

Practice Simple Conversations

Now that you know some basic greetings and introductions, let's put them together into a simple conversation:

Person A: Hallo! Wie heißt du? (Hello! What is your name?)
Person B: Ich heiße Maria. Und du? (My name is Maria. And you?)
Person A: Ich heiße John. Wie geht's? (My name is John. How are you?)
Person B: Mir geht es gut, danke! Und dir? (I'm doing well, thank you! And you?)
Person A: Auch gut, danke! (Also good, thank you!)
Person B: Tschüss! (Bye!)
Person A: Tschüss! (Bye!)

Key Points to Remember

- **Basic Greetings:** Learn different ways to say "Hello" and "Goodbye" in German.

- **Introducing Yourself:** Practice saying your name and asking for others' names.

- **Polite Phrases:** Use words like "Bitte," "Danke," and "Entschuldigung" to be polite.

- **Talking About Where You're From:** Know how to say where you come from or where you live.

- **Simple Conversations:** Combine greetings, introductions, and polite phrases to start a conversation in German.

Chapter 4

Numbers and Counting

In this chapter, we are going to learn how to count in German! Numbers are everywhere: on clocks, in books, and when you count your snacks! Knowing how to count in German is very important because it will help you understand prices, dates, time, and much more. By the end of this chapter, you will be able to count from 1 to 100, and even learn some bigger numbers. Let's get started!

Numbers from 1 to 10

We'll begin with the numbers from 1 to 10. These are the most important numbers to know because they form the building blocks for all other numbers. Here are the German numbers from 1 to 10:

- **1 – Eins** (pronounced: ayns)
- **2 – Zwei** (pronounced: tsvye)
- **3 – Drei** (pronounced: dry)
- **4 – Vier** (pronounced: feer)
- **5 – Fünf** (pronounced: fuenf)
- **6 – Sechs** (pronounced: zeks)
- **7 – Sieben** (pronounced: zee-ben)
- **8 – Acht** (pronounced: ahkht)
- **9 – Neun** (pronounced: noyn)
- **10 – Zehn** (pronounced: tsayn)

Practice saying these numbers out loud! Notice how some of the sounds are different from English. For example, "zwei" starts with a "ts" sound, and "acht" has a strong "ch" sound.

Numbers from 11 to 20

Now let's move on to the numbers from 11 to 20. These numbers also have unique names, just like in English:

- **11 – Elf** (pronounced: elf)
- **12 – Zwölf** (pronounced: tsvurf)
- **13 – Dreizehn** (pronounced: dry-tsayn)
- **14 – Vierzehn** (pronounced: feer-tsayn)
- **15 – Fünfzehn** (pronounced: fuenf-tsayn)
- **16 – Sechzehn** (pronounced: zeks-tsayn)
- **17 – Siebzehn** (pronounced: zeeb-tsayn)
- **18 – Achtzehn** (pronounced: ahkht-tsayn)
- **19 – Neunzehn** (pronounced: noyn-tsayn)
- **20 – Zwanzig** (pronounced: tsvan-tsig)

Notice how the numbers from 13 to 19 are made by combining the word for the unit (like "drei" for three) with "zehn" (ten). This is similar to English numbers like thirteen (three-ten) or fourteen (four-ten).

Counting in Tens: 20, 30, 40... to 100

Now let's learn the multiples of ten from 20 to 100. These are used when you count higher numbers:

- **20 – Zwanzig** (pronounced: tsvan-tsig)
- **30 – Dreißig** (pronounced: dry-sig)
- **40 – Vierzig** (pronounced: feer-tsig)
- **50 – Fünfzig** (pronounced: fuenf-tsig)

- **60 – Sechzig** (pronounced: zeks-tsig)
- **70 – Siebzig** (pronounced: zeep-tsig)
- **80 – Achtzig** (pronounced: ahkht-tsig)
- **90 – Neunzig** (pronounced: noyn-tsig)
- **100 – Hundert** (pronounced: hoon-dert)

These numbers are easy to remember if you know the numbers 1 to 10. For example, "Dreißig" (30) is formed from "drei" (3) with an added "-ßig" ending. Each multiple of ten follows a similar pattern, so once you learn the base numbers, it becomes easy!

Combining Numbers to Count Higher

In German, numbers from 21 to 99 are formed by combining the unit number (like "eins" for one or "zwei" for two) with the word for the tens. However, unlike in English, in German, the units come first. For example:

- **21 – Einundzwanzig** (pronounced: ayn-unt-tsvan-tsig) – Literally means "one and twenty."
- **32 – Zweiunddreißig** (pronounced: tsvye-unt-dry-sig) – Literally means "two and thirty."
- **45 – Fünfundvierzig** (pronounced: fuenf-unt-feer-tsig) – Literally means "five and forty."
- **58 – Achtundfünfzig** (pronounced: ahkht-unt-fuenf-tsig) – Literally means "eight and fifty."
- **99 – Neunundneunzig** (pronounced: noyn-unt-noyn-tsig) – Literally means "nine and ninety."

Remember, in German, the smaller number always comes before the larger one, with the word "und" (and) in between. This is a fun way to form numbers, and it's easy once you get used to it!

Counting Higher: Hundreds and Beyond

Now let's go beyond 100. German numbers in the hundreds are also formed by combining the base numbers. Here are some examples:

- **100 – Einhundert** (pronounced: ayn-hoon-dert)
- **200 – Zweihundert** (pronounced: tsvye-hoon-dert)
- **300 – Dreihundert** (pronounced: dry-hoon-dert)
- **400 – Vierhundert** (pronounced: feer-hoon-dert)
- **500 – Fünfhundert** (pronounced: fuenf-hoon-dert)

To count even higher, we just keep adding more numbers! For example:

- **365 – Dreihundertfünfundsechzig** (pronounced: dry-hoon-dert-fuenf-unt-zeks-sig) – Literally means "three hundred five and sixty."
- **782 – Siebenhundertzweiundachtzig** (pronounced: zee-ben-hoon-dert-tsvye-unt-ahkht-sig) – Literally means "seven hundred two and eighty."

Notice how the hundreds come first, followed by the smaller numbers, in the same order as in English.

Counting Thousands

Numbers in the thousands are similar to hundreds. Just add "tausend" (thousand) after the number:

- **1,000 – Eintausend** (pronounced: ayn-tow-zent)
- **2,000 – Zweitausend** (pronounced: tsvye-tow-zent)
- **10,000 – Zehntausend** (pronounced: tsayn-tow-zent)
- **100,000 – Hunderttausend** (pronounced: hoon-dert-tow-zent)

You can keep combining numbers to form even bigger ones! For example, "1,234" is "Eintausendzweihundertvierunddreißig" (one thousand two hundred four and thirty).

Key Points to Remember

- **Numbers 1-10:** Start with the basics and learn how to say each number clearly.
- **Numbers 11-20:** Remember unique names for these numbers, like "elf" for eleven and "zwölf" for twelve.

- **Counting in Tens:** Use the tens as building blocks to count higher numbers.

- **Combining Numbers:** Learn to combine units and tens with "und" to form numbers like 21 and beyond.

- **Higher Numbers:** Practice saying hundreds, thousands, and beyond by building on the basic numbers.

Chapter 5

Days, Months, and Seasons

In this chapter, we are going to learn how to talk about days, months, and seasons in German! These are important because they help us talk about our birthdays, holidays, the weather, and much more. By the end of this chapter, you will know how to say the days of the week, the months of the year, and the four seasons in German. Let's dive in!

Days of the Week

Let's start with the days of the week. In German, the days of the week are very similar to English in some ways, but they have their own unique spellings and pronunciations. Here are the days of the week in German:

- **Monday – Montag** (pronounced: mohn-tahg)

- **Tuesday – Dienstag** (pronounced: deens-tahg)

- **Wednesday – Mittwoch** (pronounced: mitt-vohkh)

- **Thursday – Donnerstag** (pronounced: dohn-ers-tahg)

- **Friday – Freitag** (pronounced: fry-tahg)

- **Saturday – Samstag** (pronounced: zams-tahg)

- **Sunday – Sonntag** (pronounced: zon-tahg)

Notice that all the days of the week in German end with "-tag," which means "day." Just like in English, the week starts with Monday (Montag) and ends with Sunday (Sonntag).

Talking About Days

When you want to talk about a specific day in German, you can use the word "am" before the day. For example:

- **Am Montag** (pronounced: am mohn-tahg) – This means "On Monday."
- **Am Freitag** (pronounced: am fry-tahg) – This means "On Friday."

If you want to say "every Monday" or "on Mondays," you can simply use the day of the week without "am." For example:

- **Montags** (pronounced: mohn-tahgs) – This means "Mondays" or "every Monday."
- **Sonntags** (pronounced: zon-tahgs) – This means "Sundays" or "every Sunday."

Months of the Year

Next, let's learn the months of the year in German. These are also quite similar to English, so they should be easy to remember! Here are the months in German:

- **January – Januar** (pronounced: yah-noo-ahr)
- **February – Februar** (pronounced: fay-broo-ahr)
- **March – März** (pronounced: mehrts)
- **April – April** (pronounced: ah-pril)
- **May – Mai** (pronounced: my)
- **June – Juni** (pronounced: yoo-nee)
- **July – Juli** (pronounced: yoo-lee)
- **August – August** (pronounced: ow-goost)
- **September – September** (pronounced: zep-tem-ber)
- **October – Oktober** (pronounced: ok-toh-ber)
- **November – November** (pronounced: noh-vem-ber)
- **December – Dezember** (pronounced: de-tsem-ber)

As you can see, many of the German months look and sound very similar to English months. This makes them easier to learn and remember!

Talking About Months

When you want to say "in" a specific month, you use the word "im" before the month in German. For example:

- **Im Januar** (pronounced: im yah-noo-ahr) – This means "In January."
- **Im Oktober** (pronounced: im ok-toh-ber) – This means "In October."

If you want to talk about something that happens every month, you can use the plural form of the month:

- **Januare** (pronounced: yah-noo-ah-re) – This means "Januaries."
- **Oktobere** (pronounced: ok-toh-be-re) – This means "Octobers."

Seasons of the Year

Now let's talk about the seasons! There are four seasons in German, just like in English. Here they are:

- **Spring – Frühling** (pronounced: froo-ling)
- **Summer – Sommer** (pronounced: zom-mer)
- **Autumn/Fall – Herbst** (pronounced: hairpst)
- **Winter – Winter** (pronounced: vin-ter)

Each season brings different weather, holidays, and activities. In Germany, for example, people enjoy celebrating spring with festivals, and winter is known for its Christmas markets and snowy weather!

Talking About Seasons

To say something happens in a specific season, you use "im" just like with months. For example:

- **Im Frühling** (pronounced: im froo-ling) – This means "In the spring."

- **Im Winter** (pronounced: im vin-ter) – This means "In the winter."

If you want to say "every spring" or "every winter," you can add an "s" to the end of the word:

- **Frühlings** (pronounced: froo-lings) – This means "every spring."
- **Winters** (pronounced: vin-ters) – This means "every winter."

Combining Days, Months, and Seasons

Now that you know how to say the days, months, and seasons in German, you can start putting them together to talk about specific dates or events. For example:

Mein Geburtstag ist am 15. Mai. (pronounced: mine geh-boorts-tahg ist am funf-tsen-ten my) – This means "My birthday is on May 15th."

Wir fahren im Sommer nach Deutschland. (pronounced: veer fah-ren im zom-mer nahkh doytch-land) – This means "We are going to Germany in the summer."

Key Points to Remember

- **Days of the Week:** Learn the seven days, which all end with "-tag" (day).
- **Months of the Year:** Remember the twelve months, many of which are similar to English.
- **Seasons of the Year:** Know the four seasons: Frühling, Sommer, Herbst, and Winter.
- **Talking About Time:** Use "am" for days and "im" for months and seasons.
- **Combining Terms:** Practice using days, months, and seasons together to talk about dates and events.

Chapter 6

Colors and Shapes

Welcome to a colorful new chapter! Colors and shapes are a big part of our daily lives – from the red of a stop sign to the round shape of a soccer ball. In this chapter, we will learn how to name different colors and shapes in German. This will help you describe things around you, talk about your favorite colors, and much more. By the end of this chapter, you'll be able to identify colors and shapes in German with ease. Let's get started!

Basic Colors in German

Let's begin by learning the most common colors in German. Colors can help you describe things, express preferences, and talk about your surroundings. Here are some of the basic colors in German:

- **Red – Rot** (pronounced: roht)
- **Blue – Blau** (pronounced: blow)
- **Yellow – Gelb** (pronounced: gelb)
- **Green – Grün** (pronounced: gruen)
- **Orange – Orange** (pronounced: oh-rahn-juh)
- **Purple – Lila** (pronounced: lee-lah)
- **Pink – Rosa** (pronounced: roh-zah)
- **Brown – Braun** (pronounced: brown)
- **Black – Schwarz** (pronounced: shvahrts)
- **White – Weiß** (pronounced: vice)
- **Gray – Grau** (pronounced: grow)

Practice saying these colors out loud! Notice how some of the German words sound quite different from their English equivalents, like "Schwarz" for black and "Weiß" for white.

Describing Objects with Colors

Now that you know the basic colors, let's learn how to use them in sentences. In German, the color usually comes after the noun it describes. Here are some examples:

- **Der Apfel ist rot.** (pronounced: dehr ahp-fel ist roht) – This means "The apple is red."

- **Das Auto ist blau.** (pronounced: das ow-toh ist blow) – This means "The car is blue."

- **Die Blume ist gelb.** (pronounced: dee bloo-meh ist gelb) – This means "The flower is yellow."

Remember that in German, every noun has a gender: masculine (der), feminine (die), or neuter (das). The article (der, die, das) affects how you describe things with colors.

Shades of Colors

Just like in English, German has words for different shades of colors. Here are some ways to talk about shades:

- **Light – Hell** (pronounced: hell)

- **Dark – Dunkel** (pronounced: doon-kel)

You can use these words to describe lighter or darker shades of a color. For example:

- **Hellblau** (pronounced: hell-blow) – This means "light blue."

- **Dunkelgrün** (pronounced: doon-kel-gruen) – This means "dark green."

Basic Shapes in German

Now that we know how to name and describe colors, let's learn the names of some basic shapes in German. Shapes help us describe objects around us, from a square window to a round clock. Here are the most common shapes:

- **Circle – Kreis** (pronounced: kryss)

- **Square – Quadrat** (pronounced: kvah-draht)

- **Rectangle – Rechteck** (pronounced: rekh-tek)
- **Triangle – Dreieck** (pronounced: dry-ek)
- **Oval – Oval** (pronounced: oh-vahl)
- **Star – Stern** (pronounced: shtairn)
- **Heart – Herz** (pronounced: herts)
- **Diamond – Raute** (pronounced: row-teh)

These shapes are all around us! Think of a "Kreis" (circle) like a coin, a "Quadrat" (square) like a picture frame, or a "Dreieck" (triangle) like a slice of pizza.

Describing Objects with Shapes

Just like with colors, you can use shapes to describe things. Here are some examples of how to use shapes in sentences:

- **Der Tisch ist rechteckig.** (pronounced: dehr tish ist rek-tek-ig) – This means "The table is rectangular."
- **Die Lampe ist rund.** (pronounced: dee lahm-peh ist roond) – This means "The lamp is round."
- **Das Fenster ist quadratisch.** (pronounced: das fen-ster ist kvah-drah-tish) – This means "The window is square."

Combining Colors and Shapes

Now that you know how to name both colors and shapes, you can combine them to describe objects more fully. For example:

- **Die rote Blume ist rund.** (pronounced: dee ro-teh bloo-meh ist roond) – This means "The red flower is round."
- **Das blaue Auto ist quadratisch.** (pronounced: das blow-eh ow-toh ist kvah-drah-tish) – This means "The blue car is square."
- **Der grüne Ball ist oval.** (pronounced: dehr grue-neh bahl ist oh-vahl) – This means "The green ball is oval."

Talking About Your Favorite Colors and Shapes

You can also use colors and shapes to talk about your favorites! Here's how to say "My favorite color is..." in German:

- **Meine Lieblingsfarbe ist...** (pronounced: my-neh leeb-lings-fahr-beh ist...) – This means "My favorite color is..."

And here's how to say "My favorite shape is...":

- **Meine Lieblingsform ist...** (pronounced: my-neh leeb-lings-form ist...) – This means "My favorite shape is..."

For example, you could say:

- **Meine Lieblingsfarbe ist blau.** (pronounced: my-neh leeb-lings-fahr-beh ist blow) – This means "My favorite color is blue."

- **Meine Lieblingsform ist der Kreis.** (pronounced: my-neh leeb-lings-form ist dehr kryss) – This means "My favorite shape is the circle."

Key Points to Remember

- **Basic Colors:** Learn the German words for common colors like rot (red), blau (blue), and gelb (yellow).

- **Describing with Colors:** Practice using colors in sentences to describe objects.

- **Basic Shapes:** Know the German names for common shapes like Kreis (circle), Quadrat (square), and Dreieck (triangle).

- **Combining Colors and Shapes:** Use both colors and shapes to describe objects more completely.

- **Favorites:** Practice talking about your favorite colors and shapes using "Lieblings."

Chapter 7

Family and Relationships

Family is an important part of everyone's life, and knowing how to talk about your family in German is a great way to start speaking the language. In this chapter, we will learn the names of different family members and how to describe relationships in German. By the end of this chapter, you will be able to introduce your family members, talk about them, and ask others about their families. Let's begin!

Basic Family Members in German

Let's start by learning the names for different family members in German. These are words you will use often when talking about your family. Here are the most common ones:

- **Mother – Mutter** (pronounced: moot-er)

- **Father – Vater** (pronounced: fah-ter)

- **Brother – Bruder** (pronounced: broo-der)

- **Sister – Schwester** (pronounced: shvest-er)

- **Grandmother – Großmutter** (pronounced: gross-moot-er) or **Oma** (pronounced: oh-mah)

- **Grandfather – Großvater** (pronounced: gross-fah-ter) or **Opa** (pronounced: oh-pah)

- **Aunt – Tante** (pronounced: tahn-teh)

- **Uncle – Onkel** (pronounced: ong-kel)

- **Cousin (male) – Cousin** (pronounced: koo-zang)

- **Cousin (female) – Cousine** (pronounced: koo-zeen-eh)

These are the basic words for family members, and they will help you describe your own family or ask about someone else's family.

Talking About Your Family

To talk about your family in German, you can use phrases like "This is..." or "My..." Here are some examples:

- **Das ist meine Mutter.** (pronounced: das ist my-neh moot-er) – This means "This is my mother."

- **Das ist mein Vater.** (pronounced: das ist mine fah-ter) – This means "This is my father."

- **Meine Schwester heißt Anna.** (pronounced: my-neh shvest-er hysst ahn-nah) – This means "My sister's name is Anna."

- **Mein Bruder ist zehn Jahre alt.** (pronounced: mine broo-der ist tsayn yah-reh ahlt) – This means "My brother is ten years old."

Notice that "mein" is used for masculine nouns like "Vater" (father) and "Bruder" (brother), while "meine" is used for feminine nouns like "Mutter" (mother) and "Schwester" (sister).

Extended Family Members

Now, let's learn some words for extended family members. These are also important when talking about family gatherings, holidays, and special events. Here are some of them:

- **Nephew – Neffe** (pronounced: nef-feh)

- **Niece – Nichte** (pronounced: nish-teh)

- **Grandson – Enkel** (pronounced: en-kel)

- **Granddaughter – Enkelin** (pronounced: en-keh-lin)

- **Son – Sohn** (pronounced: zohn)

- **Daughter – Tochter** (pronounced: tohk-ter)

Knowing these words will help you describe your extended family in more detail. For example, "Mein Neffe heißt Max" means "My nephew's name is Max."

Describing Family Relationships

To talk about how people in your family are related to each other, you can use simple phrases like these:

- **Meine Mutter ist die Schwester meines Onkels.** (pronounced: my-neh moot-er ist dee shvest-er my-nes ong-kels) – This means "My mother is my uncle's sister."

- **Mein Vater ist der Sohn meines Großvaters.** (pronounced: mine fah-ter ist dehr zohn my-nes gross-fah-ters) – This means "My father is my grandfather's son."

- **Meine Cousine ist die Tochter meiner Tante.** (pronounced: my-neh koo-zeen-eh ist dee tohk-ter my-ner tahn-teh) – This means "My cousin is my aunt's daughter."

Using these phrases, you can describe how everyone in your family is connected.

Talking About Marital Status

Sometimes, it is useful to know the words for different marital statuses in German. Here are some common terms:

- **Married – Verheiratet** (pronounced: fer-high-rah-tet)
- **Single – Ledig** (pronounced: lay-dig)
- **Divorced – Geschieden** (pronounced: geh-shee-den)
- **Widowed – Verwitwet** (pronounced: fer-vit-vet)

These words can help you describe the status of different family members. For example, "Meine Tante ist verheiratet" means "My aunt is married."

Asking About Someone's Family

When meeting someone new, it's common to ask about their family. Here are some ways to ask questions about family in German:

- **Hast du Geschwister?** (pronounced: hahst doo geh-shvist-er) – This means "Do you have siblings?"

- **Wie heißen deine Eltern?** (pronounced: vee hys-sen dy-neh el-tern) – This means "What are your parents' names?"

- **Haben Sie Kinder?** (pronounced: hah-ben zee kin-der) – This means "Do you have children?" (formal)

These questions will help you learn more about someone's family and share information about your own.

Describing Family Activities

Talking about what your family likes to do together is another great way to practice German. Here are some phrases you can use:

- **Wir gehen zusammen spazieren.** (pronounced: veer gay-en tsoo-zah-men shpa-tsee-ren) – This means "We go for a walk together."

- **Meine Familie isst oft zusammen Abendessen.** (pronounced: my-neh fah-mee-lee-eh ist oft tsoo-zah-men ah-bend-es-sen) – This means "My family often eats dinner together."

- **Wir spielen am Wochenende Fußball.** (pronounced: veer shpee-len am voh-ken-en foos-ball) – This means "We play soccer on the weekend."

These sentences help you describe common activities and things you enjoy doing with your family.

Key Points to Remember

- **Basic Family Terms:** Learn the German words for immediate family members like Mutter (mother) and Vater (father).

- **Extended Family Terms:** Practice words for extended family members like Tante (aunt) and On kel (uncle).

- **Describing Relationships:** Use phrases to explain how family members are related to each other.

- **Asking About Family:** Practice asking and answering questions about family in German.

- **Family Activities:** Learn how to talk about activities you do with your family.

Chapter 8

Common Phrases and Expressions

Now that you've learned some basic German vocabulary, it's time to dive into common phrases and expressions. These are sentences and words you can use in everyday conversations, whether you're saying "thank you," asking for directions, or making a new friend. Learning these phrases will help you feel more confident when speaking German. Let's get started!

Greetings and Farewells

Greetings are one of the most common parts of any conversation. Here are some simple ways to say hello and goodbye in German:

- **Hallo!** (pronounced: hah-loh) – This means "Hello!" and can be used in most situations.

- **Guten Morgen!** (pronounced: goo-ten mor-gen) – This means "Good morning!" and is used in the morning.

- **Guten Tag!** (pronounced: goo-ten tahk) – This means "Good day!" and is used throughout the day.

- **Guten Abend!** (pronounced: goo-ten ah-bent) – This means "Good evening!" and is used in the evening.

- **Auf Wiedersehen!** (pronounced: owf vee-der-zay-en) – This means "Goodbye!" and is a formal way to say farewell.

- **Tschüss!** (pronounced: chooss) – This is an informal way to say "Bye!"

Using these greetings and farewells will help you start and end conversations politely.

Polite Expressions

Politeness is very important in any language. Here are some polite expressions you can use in German:

- **Bitte** (pronounced: bit-teh) – This means "Please." You can use it when asking for something, like "Ein Wasser, bitte" (A water, please).

- **Danke** (pronounced: dahn-keh) – This means "Thank you." It's a simple way to show gratitude.

- **Vielen Dank** (pronounced: fee-len dank) – This means "Thank you very much." Use it when you want to express extra appreciation.

- **Entschuldigung** (pronounced: ent-shool-dee-goong) – This means "Excuse me" or "I'm sorry." You can use it to get someone's attention or apologize.

- **Kein Problem** (pronounced: kine proh-blehm) – This means "No problem." Use it when someone thanks you or when you want to show something is okay.

These expressions will help you be polite and friendly in conversations.

Basic Questions

Asking questions is a great way to learn and make friends. Here are some simple questions you can use in German:

- **Wie geht's?** (pronounced: vee gates) – This means "How are you?" It's an informal way to ask someone how they're doing.

- **Wie heißen Sie?** (pronounced: vee hys-sen zee) – This means "What is your name?" Use this in formal situations.

- **Woher kommst du?** (pronounced: voh-hair komst doo) – This means "Where are you from?"

- **Was machst du?** (pronounced: vahs mahkst doo) – This means "What are you doing?"

- **Wie spät ist es?** (pronounced: vee shpate ist ess) – This means "What time is it?"

These basic questions will help you learn more about people and practice your German skills.

Asking for Help or Directions

When traveling or in a new place, you might need to ask for help or directions. Here are some useful phrases:

- **Wo ist...?** (pronounced: voh ist...) – This means "Where is...?" For example, "Wo ist die Toilette?" means "Where is the bathroom?"

- **Können Sie mir helfen?** (pronounced: kuh-nen zee meer hel-fen) – This means "Can you help me?" Use this to ask for assistance.

- **Ich habe mich verlaufen.** (pronounced: ikh hah-beh mikh fer-low-fen) – This means "I am lost."

- **Ich brauche Hilfe.** (pronounced: ikh brow-keh hil-feh) – This means "I need help."

These phrases are very helpful when you need directions or assistance.

Making Requests and Offers

There are times when you may want to make a request or offer something to someone. Here are some phrases to help you:

- **Könnte ich bitte...?** (pronounced: kuhn-teh ikh bit-teh...) – This means "Could I please...?" For example, "Könnte ich bitte Wasser haben?" means "Could I please have some water?"

- **Möchten Sie...?** (pronounced: murkh-ten zee...) – This means "Would you like...?" For example, "Möchten Sie Tee?" means "Would you like tea?"

- **Ich hätte gern...** (pronounced: ikh heh-teh gairn...) – This means "I would like..." Use this when ordering food or drinks. For example, "Ich hätte gern einen Apfel" means "I would like an apple."

Using these phrases will help you make polite requests and offers.

Expressing Feelings and Emotions

Talking about how you feel is important in any language. Here are some common ways to express emotions in German:

- **Ich bin glücklich.** (pronounced: ikh bin gluek-likh) – This means "I am happy."

- **Ich bin traurig.** (pronounced: ikh bin trow-rikh) – This means "I am sad."

- **Ich habe Angst.** (pronounced: ikh hah-beh ahngst) – This means "I am scared."

- **Ich bin müde.** (pronounced: ikh bin myoo-deh) – This means "I am tired."

- **Ich bin aufgeregt.** (pronounced: ikh bin owf-ge-rekt) – This means "I am excited."

These expressions help you communicate your feelings and connect with others.

Responding to Questions and Statements

Knowing how to respond to questions or statements is also important. Here are some simple ways to reply in German:

- **Ja** (pronounced: yah) – This means "Yes."

- **Nein** (pronounced: nine) – This means "No."

- **Vielleicht** (pronounced: fee-lykh) – This means "Maybe."

- **Natürlich** (pronounced: nah-tuer-likh) – This means "Of course."

- **Das ist gut.** (pronounced: das ist goot) – This means "That is good."

Using these responses will help you keep conversations going and understand others better.

Key Points to Remember

- **Greetings and Farewells:** Learn how to greet people and say goodbye in different ways.

- **Polite Expressions:** Use polite phrases like "Bitte" (please) and "Danke" (thank you) to show respect.

- **Basic Questions:** Practice asking questions to learn more about others and engage in conversations.

- **Asking for Help:** Use phrases to ask for directions or assistance when needed.

- **Expressing Emotions:** Learn how to talk about your feelings to communicate more effectively.

Chapter 9

Basic Grammar: Nouns and Articles

Welcome to the world of German grammar! In this chapter, we will learn about nouns and articles, which are the building blocks of any sentence. Nouns are the names of people, places, things, or ideas, while articles are little words like "the" and "a" that go before nouns. Understanding how nouns and articles work in German will help you create simple sentences and talk about things around you. Let's get started!

What Are Nouns?

Just like in English, a noun in German is a word that names a person, place, thing, or idea. For example:

- **Person:** der Mann (the man), die Frau (the woman)

- **Place:** die Schule (the school), das Haus (the house)

- **Thing:** das Buch (the book), der Apfel (the apple)

- **Idea:** die Liebe (love), der Mut (courage)

In German, all nouns are capitalized, no matter where they appear in a sentence. This makes them easy to spot!

Gender of Nouns

One of the unique things about German is that every noun has a gender. There are three genders in German:

- **Masculine:** For male people, animals, and some objects (e.g., der Vater – the father, der Hund – the dog)

- **Feminine:** For female people, animals, and some objects (e.g., die Mutter – the mother, die Katze – the cat)

- **Neuter:** For things that are neither male nor female (e.g., das Kind – the child, das Auto – the car)

It's important to learn the gender of each noun because it will help you choose the right article to use with the noun.

Articles in German

Articles are small words that come before nouns. In English, we use "the" and "a" as articles. In German, articles change based on the gender of the noun. Here are the definite articles (meaning "the") in German:

- **Der** (pronounced: dair) – Used for masculine nouns (e.g., der Tisch – the table)
- **Die** (pronounced: dee) – Used for feminine nouns (e.g., die Blume – the flower)
- **Das** (pronounced: dahs) – Used for neuter nouns (e.g., das Haus – the house)

These articles are very important in German. Always learn the article with the noun, as it tells you the gender of the noun and helps with correct grammar.

Indefinite Articles

Just like in English, German also has indefinite articles, which mean "a" or "an." Here are the indefinite articles in German:

- **Ein** (pronounced: ayn) – Used for masculine and neuter nouns (e.g., ein Hund – a dog, ein Auto – a car)
- **Eine** (pronounced: eye-neh) – Used for feminine nouns (e.g., eine Katze – a cat, eine Schule – a school)

Remember, the indefinite article changes depending on the gender of the noun. It's important to practice and get used to using the correct article with each noun.

Plural Nouns

In German, when you talk about more than one person, place, or thing, you use plural nouns. The definite article for all plural nouns, regardless of gender, is always:

- **Die** (pronounced: dee) – Used for all plural nouns (e.g., die Hunde – the dogs, die Bücher – the books)

However, the endings of the plural forms of nouns vary. Here are a few examples of how nouns change from singular to plural:

- **Der Apfel** (pronounced: dair ap-fel) – **Die Äpfel** (pronounced: dee ep-fel) – the apples
- **Die Frau** (pronounced: dee frow) – **Die Frauen** (pronounced: dee frow-en) – the women
- **Das Kind** (pronounced: das kint) – **Die Kinder** (pronounced: dee kin-der) – the children

There is no one rule for how to make plurals in German, so it is best to learn them with the nouns. Practice will help you remember!

Using Nouns and Articles in Sentences

Now that we know about nouns and their articles, let's learn how to use them in sentences. Here are a few examples:

- **Der Hund ist groß.** (pronounced: dair hoond ist gross) – This means "The dog is big."
- **Eine Blume ist schön.** (pronounced: eye-neh bloo-meh ist shern) – This means "A flower is beautiful."
- **Das Haus ist alt.** (pronounced: das house ist ahlt) – This means "The house is old."

Notice how the article matches the gender of the noun. Practicing sentences like these will help you get used to using the right articles with the right nouns.

Exceptions to Remember

There are always exceptions to every rule, and German is no different. Some nouns may seem masculine, feminine, or neuter based on their meanings, but have a different grammatical gender. For example:

- **Das Mädchen** (pronounced: das maid-shen) – the girl (neuter, even though it refers to a female person)
- **Die Sonne** (pronounced: dee zon-neh) – the sun (feminine, even though it's an object)
- **Der Mond** (pronounced: dair mohnd) – the moon (masculine, even though it's an object)

These are just a few examples of exceptions, so it's always good to learn the gender of each noun as you go along.

How to Remember Genders and Articles

To remember which article goes with which noun, try these helpful tips:

- **Learn nouns with their articles:** When you learn a new word, always say or write it with its article (e.g., der Tisch – the table).

- **Use color coding:** Write masculine nouns in blue, feminine in red, and neuter in green to help remember their gender.

- **Practice with sentences:** Make simple sentences using nouns and their articles to get used to their correct use.

With time and practice, you'll find it easier to remember which nouns are masculine, feminine, or neuter!

Key Points to Remember

- **Nouns:** Remember that all German nouns are capitalized and can be masculine, feminine, or neuter.

- **Articles:** Learn the definite articles (der, die, das) and indefinite articles (ein, eine) for each gender.

- **Plurals:** Use die for all plural nouns and learn how nouns change from singular to plural.

- **Use in Sentences:** Practice using nouns and their articles in simple sentences to understand their gender and meaning.

- **Exceptions:** Be aware of exceptions where the gender does not match the meaning you might expect.

Chapter 10

Basic Grammar: Verbs and Tenses

Verbs are action words, like "run," "eat," or "play." They tell us what someone is doing or what is happening. In German, just like in English, verbs are an important part of sentences. Understanding how to use verbs correctly will help you talk about actions and describe things in the past, present, or future. In this chapter, we will learn some basic verbs in German and how to use them in different tenses. Let's start with the basics!

What Are Verbs?

Verbs are words that describe actions, occurrences, or states of being. For example, here are some common German verbs:

- **gehen** (pronounced: gay-hen) – to go

- **essen** (pronounced: es-sen) – to eat

- **spielen** (pronounced: shpee-len) – to play

- **lesen** (pronounced: lay-zen) – to read

- **haben** (pronounced: hah-ben) – to have

- **sein** (pronounced: zine) – to be

These verbs are used every day in German, and you will see them in many sentences. It's important to learn their meanings and how to use them correctly.

Conjugating Verbs in the Present Tense

When we use a verb in a sentence, we need to change its form to match the subject (the person or thing doing the action). This is called "conjugation." In German, verbs change their endings depending on who is doing the action. Let's start with the present tense, which is used to talk about things happening right now.

Here is how we conjugate the verb **gehen** (to go) in the present tense:

- **ich gehe** (pronounced: ikh gay-he) – I go
- **du gehst** (pronounced: doo gayst) – you go (informal)
- **er/sie/es geht** (pronounced: air/zee/es gayt) – he/she/it goes
- **wir gehen** (pronounced: veer gay-hen) – we go
- **ihr geht** (pronounced: eer gayt) – you all go (informal plural)
- **sie gehen** (pronounced: zee gay-hen) – they go

Notice how the verb endings change based on the subject. For "ich" (I), we use "-e" at the end, for "du" (you, informal) we use "-st," and so on. It's important to remember these endings to use verbs correctly in sentences.

Common Present Tense Verbs

Let's look at some more examples of verbs in the present tense:

- **Ich spiele Fußball.** (pronounced: ikh shpee-leh foos-ball) – I play soccer.
- **Du liest ein Buch.** (pronounced: doo leest ayn bookh) – You read a book.
- **Er isst einen Apfel.** (pronounced: air ist eye-nen ap-fel) – He eats an apple.
- **Wir haben einen Hund.** (pronounced: veer hah-ben eye-nen hoond) – We have a dog.
- **Sie sind glücklich.** (pronounced: zee zint gluek-likh) – They are happy.

These examples show different verbs in use. Remember to match the verb ending with the correct subject.

The Verb "Sein" (To Be)

The verb "sein" is one of the most important verbs in German. It means "to be" and is used to talk about identity, characteristics, and more. Here is how we conjugate "sein" in the present tense:

- **ich bin** (pronounced: ikh bin) – I am
- **du bist** (pronounced: doo bist) – you are (informal)
- **er/sie/es ist** (pronounced: air/zee/es ist) – he/she/it is
- **wir sind** (pronounced: veer zint) – we are
- **ihr seid** (pronounced: eer zite) – you all are (informal plural)
- **sie sind** (pronounced: zee zint) – they are

"Sein" is used very often, so it's important to memorize its forms!

Past Tense in German

Now let's learn about the past tense, which is used to talk about things that have already happened. In German, there are two main ways to express the past: the **Perfekt** (present perfect) and the **Präteritum** (simple past). For now, we will focus on the **Perfekt**, as it is more commonly used in everyday conversation.

To form the **Perfekt**, you need two parts: a helping verb (usually "haben" or "sein") and the **past participle** of the main verb. Here is how you can form the **Perfekt** for the verb "machen" (to make/do):

- **Ich habe gemacht.** (pronounced: ikh hah-beh geh-mahkt) – I made/did.
- **Du hast gemacht.** (pronounced: doo hahst geh-mahkt) – You made/did.
- **Er/sie/es hat gemacht.** (pronounced: air/zee/es haht geh-mahkt) – He/she/it made/did.
- **Wir haben gemacht.** (pronounced: veer hah-ben geh-mahkt) – We made/did.
- **Ihr habt gemacht.** (pronounced: eer hahbt geh-mahkt) – You all made/did.
- **Sie haben gemacht.** (pronounced: zee hah-ben geh-mahkt) – They made/did.

The helping verb "haben" or "sein" is conjugated according to the subject, while the past participle of the main verb stays the same.

When to Use "Haben" and "Sein" in the Past Tense

Most verbs use "haben" to form the **Perfekt**, but some verbs use "sein." Here's a simple way to remember when to use each one:

- Use **haben** (pronounced: hah-ben) for most verbs, especially those that have a direct object (like "eat" or "make").

- Use **sein** (pronounced: zine) for verbs that show movement or a change of state (like "go," "come," "become").

Here are some examples:

- **Ich bin gegangen.** (pronounced: ikh bin geh-gahng-en) – I went.

- **Er hat gegessen.** (pronounced: air haht geh-ges-sen) – He ate.

In these examples, "gehen" (to go) uses "sein" because it indicates movement, while "essen" (to eat) uses "haben."

Future Tense in German

To talk about actions that will happen in the future, German uses the **Futur** tense. To form the future tense, you use the verb "werden" (to become) along with the infinitive form of the main verb. Here is how you conjugate "werden":

- **ich werde** (pronounced: ikh vair-deh) – I will

- **du wirst** (pronounced: doo veerst) – you will (informal)

- **er/sie/es wird** (pronounced: air/zee/es veert) – he/she/it will

- **wir werden** (pronounced: veer vair-den) – we will

- **ihr werdet** (pronounced: eer vair-det) – you all will (informal plural)

- **sie werden** (pronounced: zee vair-den) – they will

Here are some examples of the future tense in action:

- **Ich werde spielen.** (pronounced: ikh vair-deh shpee-len) – I will play.

- **Du wirst lesen.** (pronounced: doo veerst lay-zen) – You will read.
- **Wir werden gehen.** (pronounced: veer vair-den gay-hen) – We will go.

Notice that "werden" is conjugated according to the subject, while the main verb stays in its infinitive form at the end of the sentence.

Key Points to Remember

- **Present Tense:** Conjugate verbs according to the subject to talk about actions happening now.
- **Past Tense:** Use the **Perfekt** tense with "haben" or "sein" and the past participle to talk about actions that have already happened.
- **Helping Verbs:** Remember when to use "haben" and "sein" in the past tense, depending on the verb's meaning.
- **Future Tense:** Use "werden" plus the infinitive form of the verb to talk about future actions.
- **Practice:** Regular practice with these tenses will help you feel more comfortable using verbs in German.

Chapter 11

Basic Grammar: Adjectives and Adverbs

Now that you have learned about nouns and verbs, it's time to add some color and detail to your sentences with adjectives and adverbs! Adjectives and adverbs make your sentences more interesting by describing nouns, pronouns, or verbs. In this chapter, we will learn what adjectives and adverbs are, how to use them in German, and why they are important. Let's get started!

What Are Adjectives?

Adjectives are words that describe or modify nouns and pronouns. They give more information about the person, place, or thing you are talking about. In English, adjectives are words like "big," "small," "happy," or "blue." Here are some common German adjectives:

- **groß** (pronounced: gross) – big
- **klein** (pronounced: kline) – small
- **schön** (pronounced: shurn) – beautiful
- **alt** (pronounced: ahlt) – old
- **jung** (pronounced: yoong) – young
- **schnell** (pronounced: shnell) – fast
- **langsam** (pronounced: lahng-zahm) – slow

These adjectives can describe many things. For example, "groß" (big) can describe a person, a building, or even a tree. Adjectives help you express what you see, feel, and think.

How to Use Adjectives in German

In German, adjectives usually come before the noun they describe, just like in English. However, they must also match the gender, number, and case of the noun they are describing. Here are some examples:

- **Der große Hund** (pronounced: dair gross-eh hoond) – The big dog (masculine)
- **Die kleine Katze** (pronounced: dee kline-eh kaht-zeh) – The small cat (feminine)
- **Das schöne Haus** (pronounced: das shurn-eh house) – The beautiful house (neuter)
- **Die alten Bücher** (pronounced: dee ahl-ten boo-kher) – The old books (plural)

Notice that the ending of the adjective changes depending on the noun's gender (masculine, feminine, or neuter) and whether it is singular or plural. It is important to learn these endings to use adjectives correctly in German.

Adjective Endings

Adjectives in German take different endings based on the definite or indefinite articles that precede them. Here is a simple guide to remember:

- **Masculine Nouns:** Add "-e" after "der" (e.g., der kleine Junge – the small boy)
- **Feminine Nouns:** Add "-e" after "die" (e.g., die schöne Blume – the beautiful flower)
- **Neuter Nouns:** Add "-e" after "das" (e.g., das rote Auto – the red car)
- **Plural Nouns:** Add "-en" after "die" (e.g., die langen Tage – the long days)

These endings help the adjective agree with the noun it describes. The more you practice, the easier it will become to remember the correct endings!

What Are Adverbs?

Adverbs are words that describe or modify verbs, adjectives, or other adverbs. They tell us more about how, when, where, or why something happens. In English, adverbs often end in "-ly," like "quickly" or "happily." Here are some common German adverbs:

- **schnell** (pronounced: shnell) – quickly
- **langsam** (pronounced: lahng-zahm) – slowly

- **heute** (pronounced: hoy-teh) – today

- **jetzt** (pronounced: yetst) – now

- **oft** (pronounced: oft) – often

- **immer** (pronounced: im-mer) – always

Adverbs add more detail to the action or situation described in the sentence. They make your descriptions clearer and more precise.

How to Use Adverbs in German

In German, adverbs usually come after the verb they modify. Let's look at some examples:

- **Er läuft schnell.** (pronounced: air loyft shnell) – He runs quickly.

- **Sie liest langsam.** (pronounced: zee leest lahng-zahm) – She reads slowly.

- **Wir kommen heute.** (pronounced: veer koh-men hoy-teh) – We are coming today.

Notice that the adverb follows the verb it describes. This is different from English, where the adverb can come before or after the verb.

Comparing Adjectives and Adverbs

Both adjectives and adverbs are used to describe, but they have different purposes. Here's a simple way to remember the difference:

- **Adjectives describe nouns:** Der Hund ist groß. (The dog is big.)

- **Adverbs describe verbs, adjectives, or other adverbs:** Der Hund läuft schnell. (The dog runs quickly.)

When you want to describe a noun, use an adjective. When you want to describe how something is done or how someone feels, use an adverb.

Forming Comparatives and Superlatives

In German, you can compare things using comparative and superlative forms, just like in English. Here's how it works:

- **Comparative:** To compare two things, add "-er" to the end of the adjective. For example:
    - **schnell** becomes **schneller** (faster)
    - **groß** becomes **größer** (bigger)
- **Superlative:** To say something is the most, use "am" before the adjective and add "-sten" to the end. For example:
    - **schnell** becomes **am schnellsten** (the fastest)
    - **klein** becomes **am kleinsten** (the smallest)

Comparatives and superlatives help you express comparisons and make your descriptions more detailed.

Using Adjectives and Adverbs in Sentences

Let's practice using adjectives and adverbs in sentences to see how they add meaning:

- **Der große Hund bellt laut.** (pronounced: dair gross-eh hoond belt lout) – The big dog barks loudly.
- **Die kleine Katze schläft ruhig.** (pronounced: dee kline-eh kaht-zeh shlaeft roo-ikh) – The small cat sleeps quietly.
- **Das rote Auto fährt schnell.** (pronounced: das ro-teh ow-toh faert shnell) – The red car drives quickly.

Notice how the adjectives (große, kleine, rote) describe the nouns (Hund, Katze, Auto), while the adverbs (laut, ruhig, schnell) describe the verbs (bellt, schläft, fährt).

Key Points to Remember

- **Adjectives:** Describe nouns and must match the gender, number, and case of the noun they modify.

- **Adverbs:** Describe verbs, adjectives, or other adverbs and usually come after the verb they modify.

- **Comparatives and Superlatives:** Add "-er" for comparisons and "am -sten" for the most.

- **Placement:** Adjectives come before nouns, and adverbs follow verbs.

- **Practice:** Use adjectives and adverbs together to make your sentences more interesting and detailed.

Chapter 12

Asking Questions in German

One of the most important things you can do when learning a new language is to ask questions. Questions help you learn more about the people around you, understand conversations, and get the information you need. In this chapter, we will learn how to ask questions in German. We will start with basic question words and then move on to how to form different types of questions. Let's get started!

Basic Question Words in German

Just like in English, German has specific words that are used to ask questions. Here are the most common question words in German:

- **Wer** (pronounced: vair) – Who
- **Was** (pronounced: vahs) – What
- **Wo** (pronounced: voh) – Where
- **Wann** (pronounced: vahn) – When
- **Warum** (pronounced: vah-room) – Why
- **Wie** (pronounced: vee) – How
- **Welcher** (pronounced: vel-kher) – Which
- **Wie viel** (pronounced: vee feel) – How much
- **Wie viele** (pronounced: vee fee-leh) – How many

These words will help you start many types of questions in German. Remember to pronounce them correctly and practice using them in sentences.

Forming Simple Questions

To ask a basic question in German, you can use one of the question words we just learned. Let's look at some examples:

- **Wer bist du?** (pronounced: vair bist doo) – Who are you?

- **Was machst du?** (pronounced: vahs mahkst doo) – What are you doing?

- **Wo wohnst du?** (pronounced: voh vohnst doo) – Where do you live?

- **Wann kommst du?** (pronounced: vahn komst doo) – When are you coming?

- **Warum lernst du Deutsch?** (pronounced: vah-room lernst doo doytch) – Why are you learning German?

- **Wie alt bist du?** (pronounced: vee ahlt bist doo) – How old are you?

Notice how the verb comes right after the question word in German. This is different from English, where the verb might come later in the question. In German, it is important to keep the word order correct to make sure your questions are understood.

Yes/No Questions

Sometimes, you only need a simple yes or no answer. In German, you can form a yes/no question by placing the verb at the beginning of the sentence. Here are some examples:

- **Bist du müde?** (pronounced: bist doo myoo-deh) – Are you tired?

- **Hast du Hunger?** (pronounced: hahst doo hoong-er) – Are you hungry?

- **Kommst du heute?** (pronounced: komst doo hoy-teh) – Are you coming today?

- **Magst du Schokolade?** (pronounced: mahkst doo shoh-ko-lah-deh) – Do you like chocolate?

To answer these questions, you can simply say **Ja** (yes) or **Nein** (no). For example, "Ja, ich bin müde" (Yes, I am tired) or "Nein, ich habe keinen Hunger" (No, I am not hungry).

Using "W-Fragen" (Question Words)

In German, questions that use question words like **wer**, **was**, **wo**, and others are called "W-Fragen" because they often start with a "w." These types of questions ask for specific information. Here are some examples using different question words:

- **Wer ist das?** (pronounced: vair ist dahs) – Who is that?

- **Was willst du essen?** (pronounced: vahs vilst doo es-sen) – What do you want to eat?

- **Wo ist die Schule?** (pronounced: voh ist dee shoo-leh) – Where is the school?

- **Wann beginnt der Unterricht?** (pronounced: vahn beh-gint dair oon-ter-rikht) – When does the lesson start?

- **Warum bist du hier?** (pronounced: vah-room bist doo heer) – Why are you here?

- **Wie viel kostet das?** (pronounced: vee feel kos-tet dahs) – How much does that cost?

These "W-Fragen" help you get specific answers, which is great when you need detailed information.

Question Word Order in German

When forming questions in German, it's important to remember that the verb always comes in the second position. Here's how to structure a question:

Question Word + Verb + Subject + Rest of the Sentence

For example:

- **Wie heißt du?** (pronounced: vee hysst doo) – What is your name?

- **Woher kommst du?** (pronounced: voh-hair komst doo) – Where are you from?

Notice how the verb "heißt" (is called) and "kommst" (come) are in the second position after the question word.

Asking for Clarification

Sometimes you may not understand something and need to ask for clarification. Here are some phrases to help you:

- **Können Sie das bitte wiederholen?** (pronounced: kuh-nen zee dahs bit-teh vee-der-ho-len) – Can you please repeat that?

- **Was bedeutet das?** (pronounced: vahs beh-doi-tet dahs) – What does that mean?

- **Wie sagt man das auf Deutsch?** (pronounced: vee zahkt mahn dahs owf doytch) – How do you say that in German?

These questions are very helpful if you are still learning and need some extra help understanding what someone is saying.

Polite Ways to Ask Questions

When asking questions, it is always good to be polite. In German, you can add "bitte" (please) to make your questions more polite. For example:

- **Können Sie mir bitte helfen?** (pronounced: kuh-nen zee meer bit-teh hel-fen) – Could you please help me?

- **Wo ist die Toilette, bitte?** (pronounced: voh ist dee toy-let-teh bit-teh) – Where is the bathroom, please?

Adding "bitte" shows respect and makes your questions sound friendlier.

Practice Questions in German

Let's practice forming some simple questions in German. Use the question words and the rules we've learned:

- **Was machst du heute?** (pronounced: vahs mahkst doo hoy-teh) – What are you doing today?

- **Wer kommt mit uns?** (pronounced: vair komt mit oons) – Who is coming with us?

- **Wann gehen wir ins Kino?** (pronounced: vahn gay-hen veer ins kee-noh) – When are we going to the movies?

Practice asking these questions out loud, and try creating your own questions using different question words!

Key Points to Remember

- **Question Words:** Learn the common German question words like "wer," "was," "wo," and others to start asking questions.

- **Word Order:** Remember that in German, the verb comes right after the question word.

- **Yes/No Questions:** Place the verb at the beginning of the sentence to form a yes/no question.

- **Politeness:** Use "bitte" to make your questions sound more polite.

- **Practice Asking:** Practice forming questions to become more comfortable speaking and understanding German.

Chapter 13

Food and Drink Vocabulary

Food and drinks are an essential part of everyday life, and knowing how to talk about them in German will be very helpful. Whether you're ordering at a restaurant, shopping for groceries, or just talking about your favorite foods, this vocabulary will come in handy. In this chapter, we'll explore common German words for different types of food and drinks, as well as some useful phrases you can use when talking about them. Let's dig in!

Basic Food Vocabulary

Let's start with some of the basic food words in German. These are common items you might eat every day:

- **das Brot** (pronounced: das broht) – bread
- **der Käse** (pronounced: dair kay-zeh) – cheese
- **die Milch** (pronounced: dee milkh) – milk
- **das Ei** (pronounced: das eye) – egg
- **das Fleisch** (pronounced: das flysh) – meat
- **das Obst** (pronounced: das ohbst) – fruit
- **das Gemüse** (pronounced: das geh-moo-zeh) – vegetables
- **der Fisch** (pronounced: dair fish) – fish
- **das Hähnchen** (pronounced: das hain-chen) – chicken
- **die Kartoffel** (pronounced: dee kar-toff-el) – potato

These words cover some of the most common foods you'll encounter. Practice saying them out loud and try to remember their genders, as this will help you use them correctly in sentences.

Fruits and Vegetables

Fruits and vegetables are an important part of a healthy diet. Here are some common fruits and vegetables in German:

- **der Apfel** (pronounced: dair ap-fel) – apple
- **die Banane** (pronounced: dee bah-nah-neh) – banana
- **die Orange** (pronounced: dee oh-rahn-geh) – orange
- **die Traube** (pronounced: dee trow-beh) – grape
- **die Tomate** (pronounced: dee toh-mah-teh) – tomato
- **die Karotte** (pronounced: dee kah-roh-teh) – carrot
- **der Salat** (pronounced: dair zah-laht) – lettuce/salad
- **die Zwiebel** (pronounced: dee tsvy-bel) – onion
- **die Gurke** (pronounced: dee goor-keh) – cucumber
- **die Paprika** (pronounced: dee pah-pree-kah) – bell pepper

These fruits and vegetables are common in German cuisine, and you might recognize some of them from your own meals. Knowing these words will help you when shopping or ordering food.

Meat, Fish, and Protein

Meat, fish, and other protein sources are also important parts of many diets. Here are some of the main words you should know:

- **das Rindfleisch** (pronounced: das rind-flysh) – beef
- **das Schweinefleisch** (pronounced: das shvine-eh-flysh) – pork
- **das Lammfleisch** (pronounced: das lahm-flysh) – lamb

- **der Schinken** (pronounced: dair shink-en) – ham

- **die Wurst** (pronounced: dee vurst) – sausage

- **der Thunfisch** (pronounced: dair toon-fish) – tuna

- **die Garnelen** (pronounced: dee gar-nay-len) – shrimp

- **die Eier** (pronounced: dee eye-er) – eggs

- **der Tofu** (pronounced: dair toh-foo) – tofu

These words will be useful when talking about meals, cooking, or even just discussing your favorite foods.

Common German Drinks

In addition to food, knowing how to talk about drinks is also important. Here are some common German words for drinks:

- **das Wasser** (pronounced: das vahs-ser) – water

- **der Saft** (pronounced: dair zaft) – juice

- **die Milch** (pronounced: dee milkh) – milk

- **der Kaffee** (pronounced: dair kah-fay) – coffee

- **der Tee** (pronounced: dair tay) – tea

- **die Limonade** (pronounced: dee lee-moh-nah-deh) – lemonade/soda

- **das Bier** (pronounced: das beer) – beer

- **der Wein** (pronounced: dair vine) – wine

- **die Schokolade** (pronounced: dee shoh-koh-lah-deh) – hot chocolate

These drinks are popular in Germany and knowing how to order them will make dining out or socializing easier.

Talking About Meals

Now that you know some basic food and drink words, let's learn how to talk about meals. Here are the names for the three main meals of the day:

- **das Frühstück** (pronounced: das froo-shtoook) – breakfast

- **das Mittagessen** (pronounced: das mitt-ag-es-sen) – lunch

- **das Abendessen** (pronounced: das ah-bend-es-sen) – dinner

You can use these words to talk about when you eat or to make plans with friends. For example:

- **Ich esse Frühstück um 8 Uhr.** (pronounced: ikh es-se froo-shtoook oom acht oor) – I eat breakfast at 8 o'clock.

- **Wir haben Mittagessen in der Schule.** (pronounced: veer hah-ben mitt-ag-es-sen in dair shoo-leh) – We have lunch at school.

- **Ich koche Abendessen für meine Familie.** (pronounced: ikh koh-khe ah-bend-es-sen foo-er my-neh fah-mee-lee-eh) – I cook dinner for my family.

These sentences will help you talk about your daily routine and meals with others.

Ordering Food and Drinks

When you're at a restaurant or café, you might need to order food and drinks. Here are some useful phrases you can use:

- **Ich hätte gern...** (pronounced: ikh heh-teh gairn...) – I would like...

- **Könnte ich bitte...haben?** (pronounced: kuhn-teh ikh bit-teh...hah-ben?) – Could I please have...?

- **Was empfehlen Sie?** (pronounced: vahs emp-fay-len zee?) – What do you recommend?

- **Die Rechnung, bitte.** (pronounced: dee rakh-noong bit-teh) – The check, please.

These phrases will help you order with confidence and be polite to the staff.

Talking About Your Favorite Foods

To talk about your favorite foods, you can use the phrase **Mein Lieblingsessen ist...** (pronounced: mine leeb-lings-es-sen ist...) – "My favorite food is...". For example:

- **Mein Lieblingsessen ist Pizza.** (pronounced: mine leeb-lings-es-sen ist pit-sah) – My favorite food is pizza.

- **Ich mag Äpfel.** (pronounced: ikh mahk ep-fel) – I like apples.

- **Ich esse gern Schokolade.** (pronounced: ikh es-se gairn shoh-koh-lah-deh) – I like to eat chocolate.

These phrases will help you share your likes and dislikes with others in German.

Key Points to Remember

- **Basic Vocabulary:** Learn common words for food and drinks like Brot (bread), Käse (cheese), and Wasser (water).

- **Meals:** Know the names for meals: Frühstück (breakfast), Mittagessen (lunch), and Abendessen (dinner).

- **Ordering Food:** Use phrases like "Ich hätte gern..." to order food politely.

- **Favorites:** Practice talking about your favorite foods with phrases like "Mein Lieblingsessen ist..."

- **Common Fruits and Vegetables:** Learn the German words for popular fruits and vegetables, such as Apfel (apple) and Tomate (tomato).

Chapter 14

Shopping and Money Vocabulary

Shopping is a great way to practice your German! Whether you are buying clothes, food, or souvenirs, knowing the right words and phrases will help you get what you need. In this chapter, we will learn common German vocabulary for shopping and handling money. You will learn how to ask for prices, sizes, and make purchases. Let's get started!

Basic Shopping Vocabulary

First, let's learn some basic words you will need when shopping:

- **das Geschäft** (pronounced: das geh-shaefft) – store/shop
- **der Laden** (pronounced: dair lah-den) – shop/store
- **der Supermarkt** (pronounced: dair zoo-per-markt) – supermarket
- **die Bäckerei** (pronounced: dee bek-er-eye) – bakery
- **die Metzgerei** (pronounced: dee metz-ger-eye) – butcher shop
- **die Apotheke** (pronounced: dee ah-po-tay-keh) – pharmacy
- **das Einkaufszentrum** (pronounced: das ein-kaufs-tsen-trum) – shopping center/mall

These words will help you understand where you are and what kind of store you are in. Practice saying them out loud to become familiar with the pronunciation.

Common Items You Might Buy

When you go shopping, it's useful to know the names of the things you might buy. Here are some common items:

- **die Kleidung** (pronounced: dee klay-doong) – clothing
- **das Hemd** (pronounced: das hemt) – shirt
- **die Hose** (pronounced: dee hoh-zeh) – pants
- **die Schuhe** (pronounced: dee shoo-heh) – shoes
- **das Kleid** (pronounced: das klite) – dress
- **der Hut** (pronounced: dair hoot) – hat
- **die Tasche** (pronounced: dee tah-sheh) – bag
- **das Buch** (pronounced: das bookh) – book
- **die Zeitschrift** (pronounced: dee tsyt-shrift) – magazine
- **die Schokolade** (pronounced: dee shoh-ko-lah-deh) – chocolate

These are just a few examples of things you might buy. Knowing these words will help you communicate with shop assistants and find what you are looking for.

Asking for Prices

When you want to know the price of something, you can use these phrases:

- **Wie viel kostet das?** (pronounced: vee feel kos-tet dahs) – How much does that cost?
- **Was kostet das?** (pronounced: vahs kos-tet dahs) – What does that cost?
- **Könnten Sie mir den Preis sagen?** (pronounced: kuhn-ten zee meer dehn prys zah-gen) – Could you tell me the price?

These questions will help you ask for prices and find out how much you need to pay.

Understanding Money in Germany

The currency used in Germany is the Euro. Here are some basic words related to money:

- **der Euro** (pronounced: dair oy-roh) – euro
- **der Cent** (pronounced: dair tsent) – cent
- **das Bargeld** (pronounced: das bar-geld) – cash
- **die Kreditkarte** (pronounced: dee kreh-deet-kar-teh) – credit card
- **die Rechnung** (pronounced: dee rekh-noong) – bill/receipt
- **der Geldautomat** (pronounced: dair geld-ow-toh-maht) – ATM

Knowing these words will help you handle money, pay for things, and manage your finances while shopping in Germany.

Making a Purchase

When you are ready to buy something, you can use these phrases:

- **Ich möchte das kaufen.** (pronounced: ikh merkh-teh dahs kow-fen) – I would like to buy that.
- **Ich nehme das.** (pronounced: ikh nay-meh dahs) – I will take that.
- **Könnte ich bitte mit Karte bezahlen?** (pronounced: kuhn-teh ikh bit-teh mit kar-teh beh-tsah-len) – Could I please pay with a card?

These phrases will help you communicate with shopkeepers and make your purchase smoothly.

Shopping for Clothes

When shopping for clothes, it's important to know how to ask for different sizes and try things on. Here are some useful phrases:

- **Welche Größe ist das?** (pronounced: vel-kheh groe-seh ist dahs) – What size is that?
- **Haben Sie das in meiner Größe?** (pronounced: hah-ben zee dahs in my-ner groe-seh) – Do you have that in my size?

- **Könnte ich das anprobieren?** (pronounced: kuhn-teh ikh dahs ahn-proh-bee-ren) – Could I try that on?

- **Wo sind die Umkleidekabinen?** (pronounced: voh zint dee oom-klai-deh-kah-bee-nen) – Where are the fitting rooms?

These phrases will help you find the right size and try on clothes when shopping.

Talking About Discounts and Sales

It's always nice to find a good deal! Here are some phrases to talk about discounts and sales:

- **Gibt es einen Rabatt?** (pronounced: gibt es eye-nen rah-baht) – Is there a discount?

- **Ist das im Angebot?** (pronounced: ist dahs im ahn-ge-boht) – Is that on sale?

- **Wie viel Prozent Rabatt gibt es?** (pronounced: vee feel pro-tzent rah-baht gibt es) – How many percent off is it?

These questions will help you find out if you can save some money on your purchases.

Returning and Exchanging Items

Sometimes, you might need to return or exchange an item. Here are some phrases to help you do that:

- **Ich möchte das umtauschen.** (pronounced: ikh merkh-teh dahs oom-tow-shen) – I would like to exchange this.

- **Kann ich das zurückgeben?** (pronounced: kann ikh dahs tsoo-rook-geh-ben) – Can I return this?

- **Wo ist der Kundendienst?** (pronounced: voh ist dair koon-den-deenst) – Where is customer service?

These phrases will help you handle any problems or exchanges while shopping in Germany.

Paying for Your Items

When you're ready to pay, you'll need to know some basic phrases to complete your purchase:

- **Wie möchten Sie bezahlen?** (pronounced: vee merkh-ten zee beh-tsah-len) – How would you like to pay?

- **Ich zahle bar.** (pronounced: ikh tsah-leh bar) – I will pay in cash.

- **Kann ich mit Kreditkarte bezahlen?** (pronounced: kann ikh mit kreh-deet-kar-teh beh-tsah-len) – Can I pay with a credit card?

- **Danke, das ist alles.** (pronounced: dahn-keh, dahs ist ah-les) – Thank you, that's all.

These phrases will help you complete your shopping experience with ease.

Key Points to Remember

- **Basic Vocabulary:** Learn common shopping words like Geschäft (store), Kleidung (clothing), and Geldautomat (ATM).

- **Asking for Prices:** Use phrases like "Wie viel kostet das?" to ask for prices.

- **Making a Purchase:** Know how to say "Ich möchte das kaufen" when you want to buy something.

- **Payment Methods:** Understand how to ask about paying with cash or a card.

- **Shopping for Clothes:** Use phrases to ask for sizes and try on clothes.

Chapter 15

Time and Dates

Understanding how to tell time and talk about dates is essential in any language. In German, just like in English, people use specific words and numbers to discuss times and dates. In this chapter, we will learn how to tell time, talk about days, months, and years, and use this knowledge to have simple conversations about schedules and events. Let's start by learning the basics!

Telling Time in German

To tell time in German, you use numbers and some key phrases. Let's begin with the most important word:

- **die Uhr** (pronounced: dee oo-er) – clock or o'clock

Here is how you can say the time in German:

- **Es ist ein Uhr.** (pronounced: es ist ayn oo-er) – It is one o'clock.
- **Es ist zwei Uhr.** (pronounced: es ist tsvy oo-er) – It is two o'clock.
- **Es ist drei Uhr.** (pronounced: es ist dry oo-er) – It is three o'clock.

And so on. Notice that "Uhr" is always used after the number to mean "o'clock."

Half Past and Quarter Past

To tell time using "half past" or "quarter past/to," here are some useful phrases:

- **Es ist halb drei.** (pronounced: es ist halb dry) – It is half past two (2:30).
- **Es ist Viertel nach vier.** (pronounced: es ist feer-tel nahkh feer) – It is a quarter past four (4:15).

- **Es ist Viertel vor fünf.** (pronounced: es ist feer-tel for fünf) – It is a quarter to five (4:45).

In German, when you say "halb drei," it literally means "half to three," which is 2:30. This is different from English, so remember this small difference!

Minutes Past and To the Hour

If you want to talk about a specific number of minutes past or to the hour, you can use these phrases:

- **Es ist zehn nach sechs.** (pronounced: es ist tsayn nahkh zeks) – It is ten past six (6:10).
- **Es ist zwanzig vor sieben.** (pronounced: es ist tsvan-tsikh for zee-ben) – It is twenty to seven (6:40).

"Nach" means "past," and "vor" means "to." These words help you specify the time in detail.

AM and PM in German

Unlike English, German does not use "AM" or "PM" to differentiate between morning and afternoon times. Instead, Germans use a 24-hour clock, especially for schedules, timetables, and formal events. Here's how it works:

- **13:00 Uhr** (pronounced: drei-zehn oo-er) – 1:00 PM
- **15:30 Uhr** (pronounced: fünf-zehn dreißig oo-er) – 3:30 PM
- **20:45 Uhr** (pronounced: zwanzig fünf-und-vierzig oo-er) – 8:45 PM

For informal conversations, people often use the 12-hour clock with words like "morgens" (in the morning), "nachmittags" (in the afternoon), and "abends" (in the evening) to clarify the time of day.

Days of the Week

Let's learn the days of the week in German:

- **Montag** (pronounced: mohn-tahg) – Monday
- **Dienstag** (pronounced: deens-tahg) – Tuesday
- **Mittwoch** (pronounced: mit-vokh) – Wednesday

- **Donnerstag** (pronounced: dohn-ers-tahg) – Thursday

- **Freitag** (pronounced: fry-tahg) – Friday

- **Samstag** (pronounced: zams-tahg) – Saturday

- **Sonntag** (pronounced: zon-tahg) – Sunday

To say "on Monday" or "on Tuesday," use the word "am" before the day:

- **am Montag** (pronounced: am mohn-tahg) – on Monday

- **am Freitag** (pronounced: am fry-tahg) – on Friday

Months of the Year

Here are the months of the year in German:

- **Januar** (pronounced: yah-noo-ar) – January

- **Februar** (pronounced: fay-broo-ar) – February

- **März** (pronounced: mehrts) – March

- **April** (pronounced: ah-pril) – April

- **Mai** (pronounced: my) – May

- **Juni** (pronounced: yoo-nee) – June

- **Juli** (pronounced: yoo-lee) – July

- **August** (pronounced: ow-goost) – August

- **September** (pronounced: zep-tem-ber) – September

- **Oktober** (pronounced: ok-toh-ber) – October

- **November** (pronounced: noh-vem-ber) – November

- **Dezember** (pronounced: de-tsem-ber) – December

To say "in January" or "in February," use the word "im" before the month:

- **im Januar** (pronounced: im yah-noo-ar) – in January

- **im Juli** (pronounced: im yoo-lee) – in July

Talking About Dates

When talking about dates in German, the day comes before the month, just like in many other countries. Here's how you can say a date:

- **der erste Januar** (pronounced: dair air-steh yah-noo-ar) – January 1st
- **der fünfte Mai** (pronounced: dair fuenf-teh my) – May 5th
- **der dreißigste Oktober** (pronounced: dair dry-sigs-teh ok-toh-ber) – October 30th

To say the date, use the word "der" (the) before the number of the day. The ending of the number changes to match the grammatical form: "erste" (first), "zweite" (second), "dritte" (third), etc.

Talking About the Year

To say the year in German, you simply read the number out loud. Here are a few examples:

- **2001** – zweitausendeins (pronounced: tsvai-tow-send-eins)
- **1999** – neunzehnhundertneunundneunzig (pronounced: noyn-tsayn-hoon-dert-noyn-oont-noyn-tsikh)
- **2023** – zweitausenddreiundzwanzig (pronounced: tsvai-tow-send-dry-oont-tsvan-tsikh)

In German, years are usually said as one whole number rather than split into two parts like in English (e.g., "nineteen ninety-nine").

Useful Phrases to Talk About Time and Dates

Here are some phrases to help you use time and dates in sentences:

- **Wie spät ist es?** (pronounced: vee shpate ist es) – What time is it?
- **Wann ist dein Geburtstag?** (pronounced: vahn ist dine geh-boorts-tahg) – When is your birthday?
- **Heute ist der dritte Juni.** (pronounced: hoy-teh ist dair drit-teh yoo-nee) – Today is the third of June.

- **Ich habe einen Termin am Montag.** (pronounced: ikh hah-beh eye-nen ter-meen am mohn-tahg) – I have an appointment on Monday.

- **Wir treffen uns um acht Uhr.** (pronounced: veer tref-fen oons oom ahkht oo-er) – We meet at eight o'clock.

Using these phrases will help you talk about time, dates, and events in everyday conversations.

Key Points to Remember

- **Telling Time:** Use "Uhr" after the number to tell time and learn phrases like "halb drei" (half past two).

- **Days and Months:** Know the days of the week and months of the year to discuss schedules and events.

- **Talking About Dates:** Remember to say the day before the month and use the correct endings.

- **24-Hour Clock:** Use the 24-hour format for formal situations and schedules.

- **Common Phrases:** Practice useful phrases to ask and answer questions about time and dates.

Chapter 16

Intermediate Grammar: Cases (Nominative, Accusative)

Welcome to learning about German grammar cases! In German, the role of a noun in a sentence is determined by its "case." This might sound new and a bit tricky, but don't worry – we will break it down step-by-step. In this chapter, we will focus on two of the four German cases: the **Nominative** and the **Accusative**. Let's learn what these cases mean and how they work!

What Are Cases in German?

In German, the case of a noun tells us how that noun is used in a sentence. Cases show if the noun is the subject, the direct object, the indirect object, or if it follows a preposition. In English, we don't change the form of nouns much, but in German, the article (like "the" or "a") and sometimes the ending of the noun change depending on the case.

There are four cases in German, but we'll start with the two most common ones:

- **Nominative** – The subject of the sentence (who or what is doing the action).
- **Accusative** – The direct object of the sentence (who or what is receiving the action).

The Nominative Case

The **Nominative** case is the "who" or "what" that is doing the action in the sentence. It is the subject of the sentence. In English, this is usually the person, animal, or thing that is "doing" the verb.

Here are the German definite articles (the word "the") in the nominative case:

- **der** (pronounced: dair) – for masculine nouns

- **die** (pronounced: dee) – for feminine nouns
- **das** (pronounced: dahs) – for neuter nouns
- **die** (pronounced: dee) – for all plural nouns

Let's look at some examples:

- **Der Hund bellt.** (pronounced: dair hoond belt) – The dog barks.
- **Die Katze schläft.** (pronounced: dee kaht-zeh shlaeft) – The cat sleeps.
- **Das Auto fährt.** (pronounced: dahs ow-toh faert) – The car drives.
- **Die Kinder spielen.** (pronounced: dee kin-der shpee-len) – The children play.

In these examples, the subjects (the dog, the cat, the car, and the children) are doing the action. So, they are in the nominative case.

The Accusative Case

The **Accusative** case is used for the direct object of a sentence. The direct object is the person, animal, or thing that is directly receiving the action of the verb. In English, we would use words like "him" or "her" to indicate the direct object.

Here are the German definite articles in the accusative case:

- **den** (pronounced: den) – for masculine nouns
- **die** (pronounced: dee) – for feminine nouns
- **das** (pronounced: dahs) – for neuter nouns
- **die** (pronounced: dee) – for all plural nouns

Notice that only the masculine article changes from **der** to **den** in the accusative case. All other articles remain the same.

Examples of the Accusative Case

Let's look at some examples to understand how the accusative case works:

- **Ich sehe den Hund.** (pronounced: ikh zay-eh den hoond) – I see the dog.
- **Sie kauft die Blume.** (pronounced: zee kowft dee bloo-meh) – She buys the flower.

- **Er hat das Buch.** (pronounced: air haht das bookh) – He has the book.

- **Wir hören die Musik.** (pronounced: veer huer-en dee moo-zeek) – We hear the music.

In these sentences, "den Hund" (the dog), "die Blume" (the flower), "das Buch" (the book), and "die Musik" (the music) are all direct objects because they are receiving the action of the verb.

How to Tell the Difference Between Nominative and Accusative

It's important to understand the difference between nominative and accusative cases. The nominative case is always the subject of the sentence – the one doing the action. The accusative case is the direct object – the one receiving the action.

Let's compare the two with some examples:

- **Der Mann isst den Apfel.** (pronounced: dair mahn ist den ap-fel) – The man eats the apple.

- In this sentence, **der Mann** is the subject (nominative), and **den Apfel** is the direct object (accusative).

- **Die Frau sieht das Kind.** (pronounced: dee frow zeet das kint) – The woman sees the child.

- In this sentence, **die Frau** is the subject (nominative), and **das Kind** is the direct object (accusative).

The key to identifying the cases is to look at who or what is performing the action (nominative) and who or what is receiving the action (accusative).

Using Articles Correctly in Sentences

To use articles correctly in German, remember these simple rules:

- For masculine nouns, use **der** in the nominative case and **den** in the accusative case.

- For feminine, neuter, and plural nouns, the articles stay the same in both the nominative and accusative cases: **die** for feminine and plural, **das** for neuter.

Here are some more examples to help you practice:

- **Der Junge spielt Fußball.** (pronounced: dair yung-eh shpee-lt foos-ball) – The boy plays soccer.

- **Ich sehe den Jungen.** (pronounced: ikh zay-eh den yung-en) – I see the boy.

Notice that "der Junge" (the boy) is in the nominative case when he is the subject, but changes to "den Jungen" in the accusative case when he is the direct object.

Key Pointers for Remembering Cases

Here are a few tips to help you remember when to use the nominative or accusative case:

- Always identify the subject (the doer) and the direct object (the receiver) in the sentence.

- For masculine nouns, pay close attention to whether you need to use "der" (nominative) or "den" (accusative).

- Practice with simple sentences and gradually build up to more complex ones.

Key Points to Remember

- **Nominative Case:** Used for the subject of the sentence – the person or thing doing the action.

- **Accusative Case:** Used for the direct object of the sentence – the person or thing receiving the action.

- **Article Changes:** Only the masculine article changes from "der" to "den" in the accusative case.

- **Identify Roles:** Always identify who or what is the subject and the direct object in a sentence.

- **Practice:** Practice with simple examples to understand the use of cases better.

Chapter 17

Intermediate Grammar: Cases (Dative, Genitive)

Now that you've learned about the Nominative and Accusative cases, it's time to explore two more cases in German: the **Dative** and **Genitive** cases. These cases are used to show different relationships between words in a sentence. Let's break them down and understand how they work!

What Are the Dative and Genitive Cases?

The Dative case is used to show the **indirect object** of a sentence – the person or thing to whom or for whom something is given or done. The Genitive case shows **possession** – it answers the question "whose?" and shows that something belongs to someone or something. Understanding these cases will help you speak and write more accurately in German.

The Dative Case

The **Dative** case is used for the indirect object in a sentence. The indirect object is usually the person or thing that is receiving something. In English, we often use words like "to" or "for" to show the indirect object, but in German, we use the Dative case.

Here are the German definite articles (the word "the") in the Dative case:

- **dem** (pronounced: dehm) – for masculine nouns
- **der** (pronounced: dair) – for feminine nouns
- **dem** (pronounced: dehm) – for neuter nouns
- **den** (pronounced: den) – for all plural nouns (Note: Add an "-n" to the end of most plural nouns in the Dative case)

Let's look at some examples:

- **Ich gebe dem Mann das Buch.** (pronounced: ikh geh-beh dehm mahn das bookh) – I give the book to the man.

- **Sie hilft der Frau.** (pronounced: zee hilt dair frow) – She helps the woman.

- **Wir danken dem Lehrer.** (pronounced: veer dank-en dehm lay-rer) – We thank the teacher.

- **Ich zeige den Kindern die Bilder.** (pronounced: ikh tsai-geh den kin-dern dee bil-der) – I show the pictures to the children.

In these sentences, the words "dem Mann" (to the man), "der Frau" (to the woman), "dem Lehrer" (to the teacher), and "den Kindern" (to the children) are all in the Dative case because they are the indirect objects receiving something.

Verbs That Commonly Use the Dative Case

Some German verbs are often used with the Dative case. Here are a few common ones:

- **helfen** (pronounced: hel-fen) – to help

- **danken** (pronounced: dank-en) – to thank

- **geben** (pronounced: geh-ben) – to give

- **schicken** (pronounced: shik-ken) – to send

- **zeigen** (pronounced: tsai-gen) – to show

These verbs often require the Dative case because they involve an indirect object (the person who receives the action).

The Genitive Case

The **Genitive** case shows possession. It is similar to using "of" or adding "'s" in English to show that something belongs to someone or something. In German, the Genitive case is less common in everyday speech but is still used in written language and formal contexts.

Here are the German definite articles in the Genitive case:

- **des** (pronounced: des) – for masculine nouns

- **der** (pronounced: dair) – for feminine nouns
- **des** (pronounced: des) – for neuter nouns
- **der** (pronounced: dair) – for all plural nouns

For masculine and neuter nouns in the Genitive case, you often add an "-s" or "-es" to the end of the noun.

Examples of the Genitive Case

Let's look at some examples to understand how the Genitive case works:

- **Das ist das Buch des Mannes.** (pronounced: das ist das bookh des mahn-nes) – That is the man's book.
- **Die Farbe der Blume ist schön.** (pronounced: dee fahr-beh dair bloo-meh ist shern) – The color of the flower is beautiful.
- **Wir besuchen die Schule des Kindes.** (pronounced: veer beh-zoo-khen dee shoo-leh des kin-des) – We visit the child's school.
- **Das Ende des Films ist spannend.** (pronounced: das en-deh des films ist shpah-nend) – The end of the movie is exciting.

In these sentences, "des Mannes" (the man's), "der Blume" (of the flower), "des Kindes" (the child's), and "des Films" (of the movie) show possession, indicating who owns or is related to the noun.

Using Articles Correctly in Sentences

To use articles correctly in German, remember these simple rules for the Dative and Genitive cases:

- For the Dative case:
    - Use **dem** for masculine and neuter nouns.
    - Use **der** for feminine nouns.
    - Use **den** for plural nouns (add "-n" to most plural nouns).

- For the Genitive case:
  - Use **des** for masculine and neuter nouns (add "-s" or "-es" to the noun).
  - Use **der** for feminine and plural nouns.

Tips for Remembering the Dative and Genitive Cases

Here are some tips to help you remember when to use the Dative or Genitive cases:

- **Dative:** Think of it as the "to/for" case – it's used for indirect objects (the person or thing receiving something).
- **Genitive:** Think of it as the "of" or "'s" case – it shows possession or ownership.
- Pay attention to the verbs that require the Dative case, like "helfen" and "danken."
- Practice identifying who owns or receives what in a sentence to know when to use each case.

Key Points to Remember

- **Dative Case:** Used for the indirect object – the person or thing receiving the action.
- **Genitive Case:** Used to show possession – indicating who or what owns something.
- **Article Changes:** Remember the changes in articles for both cases to use them correctly in sentences.
- **Common Verbs:** Learn the verbs that often use the Dative case, like "helfen" and "geben."
- **Practice:** Practice with simple examples to get comfortable using the Dative and Genitive cases.

Chapter 18

Pronouns and Possessives

Pronouns and possessives are important parts of any language. They help us talk about people, things, and who owns what without repeating the same nouns over and over. In this chapter, we will learn about German pronouns and possessives. You will learn how to use them correctly in sentences and how they change depending on their case. Let's dive in!

What Are Pronouns?

Pronouns are words that replace nouns to avoid repetition and make sentences shorter. For example, instead of saying "Anna has Anna's book," we use the pronoun "her" and say, "Anna has her book." In German, pronouns work similarly, but they change depending on the case (Nominative, Accusative, Dative, or Genitive) and the gender of the noun they replace.

Personal Pronouns in German

Let's start with the basic personal pronouns in the Nominative case, which are used as the subject of a sentence:

- **ich** (pronounced: ikh) – I
- **du** (pronounced: doo) – you (informal)
- **er** (pronounced: air) – he
- **sie** (pronounced: zee) – she
- **es** (pronounced: es) – it
- **wir** (pronounced: veer) – we
- **ihr** (pronounced: eer) – you all (informal plural)
- **sie** (pronounced: zee) – they

- **Sie** (pronounced: zee) – you (formal)

These pronouns are the subject of the sentence, meaning they are doing the action. Let's see some examples:

- **Ich lerne Deutsch.** (pronounced: ikh ler-neh doytch) – I am learning German.
- **Du spielst Fußball.** (pronounced: doo shpeelst foos-ball) – You play soccer.
- **Er trinkt Wasser.** (pronounced: air trinkt vahs-ser) – He drinks water.
- **Sie liest ein Buch.** (pronounced: zee leest ayn bookh) – She reads a book.
- **Wir gehen zur Schule.** (pronounced: veer gay-hen tsoor shoo-leh) – We go to school.

Notice how the pronoun changes to match the person doing the action. These are in the Nominative case because they are the subjects of the sentences.

Accusative Pronouns

When the pronoun is the direct object of the sentence (the one receiving the action), we use the Accusative case. Here are the pronouns in the Accusative case:

- **mich** (pronounced: mikh) – me
- **dich** (pronounced: dikh) – you (informal)
- **ihn** (pronounced: een) – him
- **sie** (pronounced: zee) – her
- **es** (pronounced: es) – it
- **uns** (pronounced: oons) – us
- **euch** (pronounced: oykh) – you all (informal plural)
- **sie** (pronounced: zee) – them
- **Sie** (pronounced: zee) – you (formal)

Here are some examples:

- **Er sieht mich.** (pronounced: air zeet mikh) – He sees me.

- **Wir lieben dich.** (pronounced: veer lee-ben dikh) – We love you.
- **Ich kenne ihn.** (pronounced: ikh keh-neh een) – I know him.
- **Sie hört uns.** (pronounced: zee hoort oons) – She hears us.

In these sentences, the pronouns "mich" (me), "dich" (you), "ihn" (him), and "uns" (us) are in the Accusative case because they are receiving the action of the verb.

Dative Pronouns

The Dative case is used for the indirect object – the person or thing receiving something indirectly. Here are the pronouns in the Dative case:

- **mir** (pronounced: meer) – to me
- **dir** (pronounced: deer) – to you (informal)
- **ihm** (pronounced: eem) – to him
- **ihr** (pronounced: eer) – to her
- **ihm** (pronounced: eem) – to it
- **uns** (pronounced: oons) – to us
- **euch** (pronounced: oykh) – to you all (informal plural)
- **ihnen** (pronounced: een-en) – to them
- **Ihnen** (pronounced: een-en) – to you (formal)

Here are some examples using the Dative case:

- **Ich gebe ihm das Buch.** (pronounced: ikh geh-beh eem das bookh) – I give him the book.
- **Sie erzählt uns eine Geschichte.** (pronounced: zee er-tsaehlt oons eye-neh ge-shikh-teh) – She tells us a story.
- **Er schenkt ihr Blumen.** (pronounced: air shenkt eer bloo-men) – He gives her flowers.
- **Wir danken Ihnen.** (pronounced: veer dank-en een-en) – We thank you (formal).

In these examples, "ihm" (to him), "uns" (to us), "ihr" (to her), and "Ihnen" (to you, formal) are in the Dative case because they are receiving something indirectly.

Possessive Pronouns

Possessive pronouns show ownership, like "my," "your," "his," "her," and so on. In German, possessive pronouns change based on the gender, number, and case of the noun they describe. Here are the basic forms:

- **mein** (pronounced: mine) – my
- **dein** (pronounced: dine) – your (informal)
- **sein** (pronounced: zine) – his/its
- **ihr** (pronounced: eer) – her/their
- **unser** (pronounced: oon-ser) – our
- **euer** (pronounced: oy-er) – your (informal plural)
- **Ihr** (pronounced: eer) – your (formal)

Let's see some examples:

- **Das ist mein Hund.** (pronounced: das ist mine hoond) – That is my dog.
- **Wo ist dein Auto?** (pronounced: voh ist dine ow-toh) – Where is your car?
- **Sein Buch ist interessant.** (pronounced: zine bookh ist in-teh-re-sanht) – His book is interesting.
- **Unsere Schule ist groß.** (pronounced: oon-zeh-re shoo-leh ist gross) – Our school is big.

In these examples, the possessive pronouns "mein" (my), "dein" (your), "sein" (his), and "unsere" (our) show who owns the dog, car, book, or school.

Using Pronouns and Possessives in Sentences

To use pronouns and possessives correctly in German, remember these key points:

- Choose the right pronoun based on the gender, number, and case of the noun.

- Use possessive pronouns to show ownership, and adjust them based on the gender and number of the noun they describe.

- Practice using pronouns and possessives in different sentences to understand how they change depending on their role.

Key Points to Remember

- **Personal Pronouns:** Learn the different pronouns in the Nominative, Accusative, and Dative cases.

- **Accusative Pronouns:** Used for the direct object – the person or thing receiving the action directly.

- **Dative Pronouns:** Used for the indirect object – the person or thing receiving something indirectly.

- **Possessive Pronouns:** Show ownership and change based on gender, number, and case.

- **Practice:** Use these pronouns in sentences to become familiar with their forms and uses.

Chapter 19

Prepositions and Conjunctions

Prepositions and conjunctions are small words that make a big difference in your sentences. They help you connect ideas, show relationships between things, and make your sentences clearer. In this chapter, we will learn about the most common German prepositions and conjunctions, how to use them, and see some examples to help you understand how they work. Let's get started!

What Are Prepositions?

Prepositions are words that show the relationship between a noun or pronoun and other words in a sentence. They often tell us where something is, when something happens, or how something is done. In German, prepositions can affect the case of the noun or pronoun that follows them. This might sound complicated, but we will go through it step-by-step.

Common Prepositions in German

Here are some of the most common German prepositions:

- **auf** (pronounced: owf) – on
- **in** (pronounced: in) – in
- **an** (pronounced: ahn) – at, on
- **unter** (pronounced: oon-ter) – under
- **über** (pronounced: ue-ber) – over, above
- **neben** (pronounced: nay-ben) – next to
- **vor** (pronounced: fohr) – in front of
- **hinter** (pronounced: hin-ter) – behind

- **zwischen** (pronounced: tsvish-en) – between

- **mit** (pronounced: mit) – with

- **nach** (pronounced: nahkh) – after, to

- **zu** (pronounced: tsoo) – to

These prepositions are used in everyday German to describe the location, direction, and time. Let's look at some examples to see how they are used in sentences:

- **Das Buch liegt auf dem Tisch.** (pronounced: das bookh leeght owf dehm tish) – The book is lying on the table.

- **Wir gehen in die Schule.** (pronounced: veer gay-en in dee shoo-leh) – We are going to the school.

- **Der Hund sitzt neben dem Auto.** (pronounced: dair hoond zitzt nay-ben dehm ow-toh) – The dog is sitting next to the car.

- **Ich fahre nach Hause.** (pronounced: ikh fah-reh nahkh how-zeh) – I am driving home.

Notice how the prepositions help describe the location (on the table, next to the car) and the direction (to the school, home).

Prepositions and Cases

In German, some prepositions always take a specific case (Accusative or Dative). Here are some examples:

- **Accusative Prepositions:** bis (until), durch (through), für (for), gegen (against), ohne (without), um (around)

- **Dative Prepositions:** aus (from, out of), bei (at, near), mit (with), nach (to, after), seit (since), von (from, of), zu (to)

Let's look at examples of prepositions that take the Accusative case:

- **Ich gehe durch den Park.** (pronounced: ikh geh-eh doorkh den park) – I am going through the park.

- **Wir spielen gegen die Mannschaft.** (pronounced: veer shpee-len gay-gen dee manns-shaft) – We are playing against the team.

And here are examples of prepositions that take the Dative case:

- **Er wohnt bei seinen Eltern.** (pronounced: air vohnt by zay-nen el-tern) – He lives with his parents.

- **Ich fahre mit dem Bus.** (pronounced: ikh fah-reh mit dehm boos) – I travel by bus.

Knowing which prepositions go with which cases will help you form correct sentences in German.

What Are Conjunctions?

Conjunctions are words that join sentences, phrases, or words together. They help connect ideas and make your sentences flow better. In German, just like in English, conjunctions can be coordinating or subordinating.

Coordinating Conjunctions

Coordinating conjunctions connect words or sentences that are of equal importance. Here are some common coordinating conjunctions in German:

- **und** (pronounced: oont) – and

- **aber** (pronounced: ah-ber) – but

- **oder** (pronounced: oh-der) – or

- **denn** (pronounced: denn) – because

- **sondern** (pronounced: zon-dern) – but rather

Let's see some examples of coordinating conjunctions in sentences:

- **Ich spiele Fußball, und du spielst Tennis.** (pronounced: ikh shpee-leh foos-ball, oont doo shpeelst te-nis) – I play soccer, and you play tennis.

- **Er kommt nicht, aber sie kommt.** (pronounced: air komt nikht, ah-ber zee komt) – He is not coming, but she is coming.

- **Möchtest du Tee oder Kaffee?** (pronounced: moekh-test doo tay oh-der kah-fay) – Would you like tea or coffee?

These conjunctions do not change the word order of the sentence in German, just like in English.

Subordinating Conjunctions

Subordinating conjunctions connect a main clause with a dependent clause. The dependent clause gives extra information about the main clause. Here are some common subordinating conjunctions in German:

- **weil** (pronounced: vile) – because
- **dass** (pronounced: dass) – that
- **wenn** (pronounced: venn) – if, when
- **obwohl** (pronounced: op-vol) – although
- **während** (pronounced: veh-rend) – while

Let's see some examples using subordinating conjunctions:

- **Ich bleibe zu Hause, weil es regnet.** (pronounced: ikh bly-beh tsoo how-zeh, vile es rayg-net) – I stay at home because it is raining.
- **Er weiß, dass sie kommt.** (pronounced: air veys, dass zee komt) – He knows that she is coming.
- **Wir spielen draußen, wenn das Wetter schön ist.** (pronounced: veer shpee-len drow-sen, venn das vet-ter shern ist) – We play outside when the weather is nice.

Note that in German, when using a subordinating conjunction, the verb moves to the end of the dependent clause. This is different from English, where the verb usually stays in its normal position.

Using Prepositions and Conjunctions Together

Prepositions and conjunctions often work together to create complex sentences that give more information. Here's an example combining both:

- **Wir gehen in den Park, weil das Wetter gut ist.** (pronounced: veer gay-en in den park, vile das vet-ter goot ist) – We are going to the park because the weather is good.

In this sentence, "in" is the preposition showing direction, and "weil" is the conjunction explaining why they are going to the park.

Key Points to Remember

- **Prepositions:** Show relationships between nouns and other words, such as location or direction.

- **Cases:** Remember that some prepositions require the Accusative or Dative case.

- **Coordinating Conjunctions:** Join words or sentences of equal importance and do not change word order.

- **Subordinating Conjunctions:** Connect a main clause with a dependent clause and change the word order in German.

- **Practice:** Use prepositions and conjunctions in sentences to understand how they change the meaning and structure.

Chapter 20

Describing People and Things

Being able to describe people and things is an important skill in any language. Descriptions help you share more information about how someone or something looks, feels, or behaves. In German, just like in English, we use adjectives and specific phrases to describe people and objects. In this chapter, you will learn some common German adjectives and how to use them to describe people and things. Let's start with the basics!

Basic Adjectives for Descriptions

Adjectives are words that describe nouns. They tell us more about a person, place, or thing. Here are some common German adjectives that are used to describe people and things:

- **groß** (pronounced: gross) – big, tall
- **klein** (pronounced: kline) – small, short
- **jung** (pronounced: yoong) – young
- **alt** (pronounced: ahlt) – old
- **schön** (pronounced: shurn) – beautiful, nice
- **hässlich** (pronounced: hes-likh) – ugly
- **freundlich** (pronounced: froynd-likh) – friendly
- **müde** (pronounced: myoo-deh) – tired
- **stark** (pronounced: shtark) – strong
- **schwach** (pronounced: shvahkh) – weak

These adjectives help you describe people's appearance and personality, as well as things around you. Let's see how to use them in sentences.

Using Adjectives to Describe People

When you describe a person in German, you can use adjectives to talk about their appearance, personality, or mood. Here are some examples:

- **Er ist groß und stark.** (pronounced: air ist gross oont shtark) – He is tall and strong.

- **Sie ist klein, aber sehr freundlich.** (pronounced: zee ist kline, ah-ber zair froynd-likh) – She is small but very friendly.

- **Das Mädchen ist jung und schön.** (pronounced: das made-khen ist yoong oont shurn) – The girl is young and beautiful.

- **Der Junge ist müde.** (pronounced: dair yung-eh ist myoo-deh) – The boy is tired.

In these sentences, the adjectives "groß" (tall), "freundlich" (friendly), "jung" (young), and "müde" (tired) describe the people being talked about. Notice how the adjectives are placed before the noun they describe.

Describing Things

Adjectives are also used to describe objects, animals, or anything else. Here are some examples of how to describe things:

- **Das Auto ist schnell.** (pronounced: das ow-toh ist shnell) – The car is fast.

- **Der Baum ist alt.** (pronounced: dair bowm ist ahlt) – The tree is old.

- **Die Blume ist schön.** (pronounced: dee bloo-meh ist shurn) – The flower is beautiful.

- **Das Buch ist interessant.** (pronounced: das bookh ist in-teh-re-sanht) – The book is interesting.

These sentences use adjectives like "schnell" (fast), "alt" (old), "schön" (beautiful), and "interessant" (interesting) to describe objects and things.

Adjective Endings in German

In German, the ending of an adjective can change depending on the gender (masculine, feminine, neuter), the number (singular or plural), and the case (Nominative, Accusative, Dative, or Genitive) of the noun it describes. Here are some simple rules:

- For **masculine** nouns in the Nominative case, add "-e" (e.g., der große Mann – the tall man).

- For **feminine** nouns in the Nominative case, add "-e" (e.g., die kleine Katze – the small cat).

- For **neuter** nouns in the Nominative case, add "-e" (e.g., das rote Auto – the red car).

- For **plural** nouns in the Nominative case, add "-en" (e.g., die alten Bücher – the old books).

Let's see these endings in action:

- **Der kleine Hund** (pronounced: dair kline hoond) – The small dog (masculine)

- **Die große Blume** (pronounced: dee gross-eh bloo-meh) – The big flower (feminine)

- **Das blaue Meer** (pronounced: das blow-eh mare) – The blue sea (neuter)

- **Die langen Straßen** (pronounced: dee lahng-en shtrah-sen) – The long streets (plural)

By learning these endings, you can use adjectives correctly to match the noun's gender, number, and case.

Using Colors to Describe Things

Colors are a great way to describe things. Here are some common colors in German:

- **rot** (pronounced: roht) – red

- **blau** (pronounced: blow) – blue

- **grün** (pronounced: gruen) – green

- **gelb** (pronounced: gelb) – yellow

- **weiß** (pronounced: vice) – white

- **schwarz** (pronounced: shvahrts) – black

- **braun** (pronounced: brow-n) – brown

- **orange** (pronounced: oh-rahn-j) – orange

Here's how to use them in sentences:

- **Das Auto ist rot.** (pronounced: das ow-toh ist roht) – The car is red.
- **Der Stuhl ist blau.** (pronounced: dair shtool ist blow) – The chair is blue.
- **Die Katze ist schwarz.** (pronounced: dee kaht-zeh ist shvahrts) – The cat is black.
- **Der Hund ist weiß.** (pronounced: dair hoond ist vice) – The dog is white.

Using colors helps make your descriptions more vivid and clear.

Describing Sizes and Quantities

To describe the size and quantity of things, you can use these adjectives:

- **groß** (pronounced: gross) – big
- **klein** (pronounced: kline) – small
- **viel** (pronounced: feel) – much, many
- wenig (pronounced: veh-nikh) – little, few

Here are some examples:

- Der Baum ist groß. (pronounced: dair bowm ist gross) – The tree is big.
- Das Haus ist klein. (pronounced: das hows ist kline) – The house is small.
- Ich habe viele Bücher. (pronounced: ikh hah-beh fee-leh boo-kher) – I have many books.
- Es gibt wenig Wasser. (pronounced: es gibt veh-nikh vahs-ser) – There is little water.

Using size and quantity words helps you give more details about what you are describing.

Key Points to Remember

- Adjectives: Use adjectives to describe people and things, such as "groß" (big) or "schön" (beautiful).
- Colors: Learn color adjectives like "rot" (red) and "blau" (blue) to describe objects vividly.

- Adjective Endings: Remember that adjective endings change based on gender, number, and case.

- Sizes and Quantities: Use words like "groß" (big), "klein" (small), "viel" (many), and "wenig" (few) to describe sizes and amounts.

- Practice: Try using adjectives in sentences to describe people, places, and things around you.

Chapter 21

Travel and Transportation Vocabulary

When traveling, it is important to know the right words to help you find your way, use public transport, and talk about different places. In this chapter, we will learn useful German vocabulary related to travel and transportation. This will help you when you are on the go, whether you're taking a bus, train, or plane, or just exploring a new city. Let's begin with some basics!

Common Transportation Words

First, let's learn some common German words for different types of transportation:

- **das Auto** (pronounced: das ow-toh) – car
- **der Bus** (pronounced: dair boos) – bus
- **der Zug** (pronounced: dair tsoog) – train
- **die Straßenbahn** (pronounced: dee shtrah-sen-bahn) – tram
- **das Fahrrad** (pronounced: das fah-rahdt) – bicycle
- **das Flugzeug** (pronounced: das floog-tsoyk) – airplane
- **das Taxi** (pronounced: das tak-see) – taxi
- **das Schiff** (pronounced: das shiff) – ship
- **die U-Bahn** (pronounced: dee oo-bahn) – subway

These words will help you talk about different ways to get around when traveling. Let's see how to use them in sentences.

Using Transportation Words in Sentences

Now that you know some basic words, let's learn how to use them in sentences:

- **Ich fahre mit dem Auto zur Schule.** (pronounced: ikh fah-reh mit dehm ow-toh tsoor shoo-leh) – I go to school by car.

- **Wir nehmen den Bus zum Bahnhof.** (pronounced: veer nay-men den boos tsoom bahn-hohf) – We take the bus to the train station.

- **Sie fliegt mit dem Flugzeug nach Berlin.** (pronounced: zee flee-gt mit dehm floog-tsoyk nahkh ber-leen) – She flies to Berlin by airplane.

- **Er fährt Fahrrad im Park.** (pronounced: air fehrt fah-rahdt im park) – He rides a bicycle in the park.

Notice how these sentences use transportation words to describe how people travel from one place to another.

Important Places for Travel

When traveling, you'll need to know the names of important places related to transportation. Here are some common German words for these places:

- **der Flughafen** (pronounced: dair floog-hah-fen) – airport

- **der Bahnhof** (pronounced: dair bahn-hohf) – train station

- **die Haltestelle** (pronounced: dee hal-te-shtel-leh) – stop (bus stop, tram stop)

- **der Hafen** (pronounced: dair hah-fen) – harbor, port

- **die Tankstelle** (pronounced: dee tank-shtel-leh) – gas station

- **die Autobahn** (pronounced: dee ow-toh-bahn) – highway

- **das Reisebüro** (pronounced: das ray-zeh-byoo-roh) – travel agency

- **der Fahrkartenautomat** (pronounced: dair fahr-kar-ten ow-toh-maht) – ticket machine

Knowing these words will help you find your way around and locate important places when traveling.

Common Travel Phrases

Here are some useful phrases to help you while traveling in a German-speaking country:

- **Wie komme ich zum Flughafen?** (pronounced: vee kohm-meh ikh tsoom floog-hah-fen) – How do I get to the airport?

- **Wo ist der Bahnhof?** (pronounced: voh ist dair bahn-hohf) – Where is the train station?

- **Wann fährt der nächste Zug?** (pronounced: vahn fehrt dair nekh-ste tsoog) – When does the next train leave?

- **Ich möchte eine Fahrkarte nach München, bitte.** (pronounced: ikh merkh-teh eye-neh fahr-kar-teh nahkh mün-khen, bit-teh) – I would like a ticket to Munich, please.

- **Gibt es hier ein Taxi?** (pronounced: gibt es heer ayn tak-see) – Is there a taxi here?

These phrases can help you ask for directions, buy tickets, or find out important information while traveling.

Describing Directions

When you are traveling, you might need to ask for directions or understand where something is located. Here are some common words and phrases to help you describe directions in German:

- **links** (pronounced: links) – left

- **rechts** (pronounced: rekhts) – right

- **geradeaus** (pronounced: geh-rah-deh-ows) – straight ahead

- **zurück** (pronounced: tsoo-ruhk) – back

- **hier** (pronounced: heer) – here

- **dort** (pronounced: dort) – there

Here are some phrases using these words:

- **Gehen Sie links.** (pronounced: geh-en zee links) – Go left.

- **Fahren Sie geradeaus.** (pronounced: fahr-en zee geh-rah-deh-ows) – Drive straight ahead.

- **Der Bahnhof ist dort.** (pronounced: dair bahn-hohf ist dort) – The train station is there.

These words and phrases will help you understand and give directions while traveling.

Buying Tickets and Asking About Prices

Knowing how to ask about prices and buy tickets is very important when using public transport. Here are some phrases to help you:

- **Wie viel kostet eine Fahrkarte?** (pronounced: vee feel kos-tet eye-neh fahr-kar-teh) – How much is a ticket?

- **Kann ich eine Rückfahrkarte haben?** (pronounced: kann ikh eye-neh rook-fahr-kar-teh hah-ben) – Can I have a return ticket?

- **Ich brauche eine Fahrkarte nach Berlin.** (pronounced: ikh brow-kheh eye-neh fahr-kar-teh nahkh ber-leen) – I need a ticket to Berlin.

- **Wo kann ich Tickets kaufen?** (pronounced: voh kann ikh tik-kets kow-fen) – Where can I buy tickets?

These phrases will help you purchase tickets and find out the cost of travel.

Understanding Timetables and Schedules

When traveling, you'll need to understand timetables and schedules to plan your journey. Here are some words and phrases that can help:

- **der Fahrplan** (pronounced: dair fahr-pl ahn) – timetable, schedule

- **die Abfahrt** (pronounced: dee ahb-fahrt) – departure

- **die Ankunft** (pronounced: dee an-kunft) – arrival

- **der Zug fährt um 10 Uhr ab.** (pronounced: dair tsoog fehrt oom tsayn oo-er ahb) – The train departs at 10 o'clock.

- **Die Ankunft ist um 12 Uhr.** (pronounced: dee an-kunft ist oom zwölf oo-er) – The arrival is at 12 o'clock.

Knowing these words will help you read schedules and plan your trips effectively.

Key Points to Remember

- **Transportation Words:** Learn basic words like "Auto" (car), "Bus," and "Zug" (train) to talk about different types of transport.

- **Travel Phrases:** Use phrases like "Wie komme ich zum Flughafen?" to ask for directions and information.

- **Describing Directions:** Understand words like "links" (left) and "rechts" (right) to give or follow directions.

- **Buying Tickets:** Know how to ask about prices and purchase tickets using phrases like "Wie viel kostet eine Fahrkarte?"

- **Timetables and Schedules:** Learn words related to schedules like "Abfahrt" (departure) and "Ankunft" (arrival) to plan your journey.

Chapter 22

Housing and Accommodation Vocabulary

When you travel or move to a new place, you need to know the right words to talk about where you live and where you stay. In this chapter, we will learn useful German vocabulary related to housing and accommodation. These words will help you describe different types of homes, rooms, and furniture, and talk about renting or booking a place to stay. Let's start with some basic terms!

Types of Housing

First, let's learn some common German words for different types of housing and places where people live:

- **das Haus** (pronounced: das hows) – house

- **die Wohnung** (pronounced: dee voh-noong) – apartment

- **das Zimmer** (pronounced: das tsim-mer) – room

- **das Einfamilienhaus** (pronounced: das ayn-fah-meel-yen-hows) – single-family house

- **die Villa** (pronounced: dee vil-lah) – villa

- **das Reihenhaus** (pronounced: das ry-en-hows) – townhouse

- **das Hochhaus** (pronounced: das hohkh-hows) – high-rise building

- **die WG (Wohngemeinschaft)** (pronounced: dee vay-gay (vohn-ge-mine-shahft)) – shared apartment

- **das Studentenwohnheim** (pronounced: das shtoo-den-ten-vohn-hyme) – student dormitory

These words will help you identify different types of homes and living arrangements. Let's see how to use them in sentences.

Using Housing Words in Sentences

Here are some examples of how to use these housing words in sentences:

- **Ich wohne in einem Haus.** (pronounced: ikh voh-neh in ayn-em hows) – I live in a house.

- **Sie wohnt in einer Wohnung.** (pronounced: zee vohnt in eye-ner voh-noong) – She lives in an apartment.

- **Wir suchen eine WG.** (pronounced: veer zoo-khen eye-neh vay-gay) – We are looking for a shared apartment.

- **Er lebt in einem Studentenwohnheim.** (pronounced: air lebt in ayn-em shtoo-den-ten-vohn-hyme) – He lives in a student dormitory.

These sentences show how to use different words to describe where you or someone else lives.

Rooms in a House or Apartment

Next, let's learn the German words for different rooms you might find in a house or apartment:

- **das Schlafzimmer** (pronounced: das shlahf-tsim-mer) – bedroom

- **das Wohnzimmer** (pronounced: das vohn-tsim-mer) – living room

- **die Küche** (pronounced: dee ku-khe) – kitchen

- **das Badezimmer** (pronounced: das bah-de-tsim-mer) – bathroom

- **das Esszimmer** (pronounced: das ess-tsim-mer) – dining room

- **der Flur** (pronounced: dair floor) – hallway

- **der Balkon** (pronounced: dair bal-kohn) – balcony

- **der Keller** (pronounced: dair kel-ler) – basement

- **der Garten** (pronounced: dair gahr-ten) – garden

These words will help you describe the different rooms in your house or apartment. Let's see some examples of how to use them in sentences:

- **Das Schlafzimmer ist groß.** (pronounced: das shlahf-tsim-mer ist gross) – The bedroom is big.
- **Die Küche ist klein, aber gemütlich.** (pronounced: dee ku-khe ist kline, ah-ber geh-muet-likh) – The kitchen is small, but cozy.
- **Wir essen im Esszimmer.** (pronounced: veer ess-en im ess-tsim-mer) – We eat in the dining room.
- **Es gibt einen Balkon und einen Garten.** (pronounced: es gibt ayn-en bal-kohn oont ayn-en gahr-ten) – There is a balcony and a garden.

These sentences show how you can talk about different rooms in a house or apartment.

Furniture and Items in the Home

Now, let's learn some German words for common furniture and items you might find in a house or apartment:

- **das Bett** (pronounced: das bet) – bed
- **der Tisch** (pronounced: dair tish) – table
- **der Stuhl** (pronounced: dair shtool) – chair
- **die Couch** (pronounced: dee kowtch) – couch
- **der Schrank** (pronounced: dair shrahngk) – cupboard/closet
- **die Lampe** (pronounced: dee lahm-peh) – lamp
- **der Teppich** (pronounced: dair tep-pikh) – rug/carpet
- **die Badewanne** (pronounced: dee bah-deh-vah-neh) – bathtub
- **der Kühlschrank** (pronounced: dair kewl-shrank) – refrigerator

Here are some sentences using these furniture words:

- **Das Bett ist sehr bequem.** (pronounced: das bet ist zair beh-kvame) – The bed is very comfortable.

- **Ich brauche einen neuen Tisch.** (pronounced: ikh brow-kheh ayn-en noy-en tish) – I need a new table.

- **Die Couch ist rot.** (pronounced: dee kowtch ist roht) – The couch is red.

- **Der Kühlschrank ist voll.** (pronounced: dair kewl-shrank ist foll) – The refrigerator is full.

These sentences show how to talk about the different pieces of furniture and items in a home.

Talking About Renting or Booking a Place

If you are looking for a place to rent or book, you need to know some important words and phrases. Here are some useful terms in German:

- **mieten** (pronounced: mee-ten) – to rent

- **vermieten** (pronounced: fer-mee-ten) – to rent out

- **die Miete** (pronounced: dee mee-teh) – rent (the payment)

- **das Zimmer frei** (pronounced: das tsim-mer fry) – room available

- **der Vertrag** (pronounced: dair fer-trahg) – contract

- **die Kaution** (pronounced: dee kow-ts yo-on) – deposit

- **die Unterkunft** (pronounced: dee oon-ter-koomft) – accommodation

- **die Buchung** (pronounced: dee boo-khoong) – booking

Here are some sentences to help you talk about renting or booking a place:

- **Wir möchten ein Zimmer mieten.** (pronounced: veer merkh-ten ayn tsim-mer mee-ten) – We would like to rent a room.

- **Gibt es hier ein Zimmer frei?** (pronounced: gibt es heer ayn tsim-mer fry) – Is there a room available here?

- **Ich habe die Buchung bestätigt.** (pronounced: ikh hah-beh dee boo-khoong beshtay-tigt) – I have confirmed the booking.

- **Die Miete ist zu hoch.** (pronounced: dee mee-teh ist tsoo hohkh) – The rent is too high.

These phrases will help you communicate effectively when renting or booking accommodation in German.

Key Points to Remember

- **Types of Housing:** Learn words like "Haus" (house) and "Wohnung" (apartment) to talk about different types of homes.

- **Rooms in a House:** Know the names of different rooms such as "Schlafzimmer" (bedroom) and "Küche" (kitchen).

- **Furniture:** Learn common furniture words like "Bett" (bed) and "Tisch" (table) to describe items in a home.

- **Renting or Booking:** Use phrases like "Wir möchten ein Zimmer mieten" to talk about renting or booking a place.

- **Accommodation Terms:** Understand terms like "die Miete" (rent) and "die Kaution" (deposit) to discuss renting and booking.

Chapter 23

Health and Body Vocabulary

Knowing how to talk about your body and health is very important, especially when you are feeling unwell or visiting a doctor. In this chapter, we will learn the basic German vocabulary related to parts of the body and health. You will also learn useful phrases that you can use when talking about how you feel or if you need help. Let's start with some essential words!

Parts of the Body

First, let's learn the names of some basic parts of the body in German:

- **der Kopf** (pronounced: dair kopf) – head
- **das Gesicht** (pronounced: das geh-zikht) – face
- **das Auge** (pronounced: das ow-geh) – eye
- **das Ohr** (pronounced: das ohr) – ear
- **die Nase** (pronounced: dee nah-zeh) – nose
- **der Mund** (pronounced: dair moond) – mouth
- **der Zahn** (pronounced: dair tsahn) – tooth
- **der Hals** (pronounced: dair hals) – neck
- **der Arm** (pronounced: dair ahrm) – arm
- **die Hand** (pronounced: dee hahnd) – hand
- **der Finger** (pronounced: dair fin-ger) – finger
- **das Bein** (pronounced: das byn) – leg

- **der Fuß** (pronounced: dair foos) – foot
- **der Rücken** (pronounced: dair ruek-ken) – back
- **der Bauch** (pronounced: dair bowkh) – stomach

These are some of the main body parts that you should know. Let's see how to use these words in sentences.

Using Body Parts in Sentences

Here are some examples of how to use the body parts in sentences:

- **Mein Kopf tut weh.** (pronounced: mine kopf toot vay) – My head hurts.
- **Er hat blaue Augen.** (pronounced: air haht blow-eh ow-gen) – He has blue eyes.
- **Sie wäscht ihre Hände.** (pronounced: zee vesht ee-reh hen-deh) – She washes her hands.
- **Ich habe Schmerzen im Rücken.** (pronounced: ikh hah-beh shmairt-sen im ruek-ken) – I have pain in my back.

These sentences show how you can talk about different parts of your body in German.

Basic Health Vocabulary

Now, let's learn some common German words and phrases related to health and well-being:

- **die Gesundheit** (pronounced: dee ge-zund-hite) – health
- **krank** (pronounced: krangk) – sick
- **gesund** (pronounced: geh-zund) – healthy
- **die Krankheit** (pronounced: dee krang-kite) – illness
- **das Fieber** (pronounced: das fee-ber) – fever
- **der Schmerz** (pronounced: dair shmairtz) – pain
- **die Grippe** (pronounced: dee grip-peh) – flu
- **die Erkältung** (pronounced: dee er-kel-toong) – cold

- **der Husten** (pronounced: dair hoo-sten) – cough

- **das Medikament** (pronounced: das may-dee-ka-ment) – medicine

- **die Tablette** (pronounced: dee tah-ble-teh) – tablet, pill

- **die Salbe** (pronounced: dee zahl-beh) – ointment

These words are helpful when you need to talk about your health or describe how you feel. Let's see how to use them in sentences:

- **Ich bin krank.** (pronounced: ikh bin krangk) – I am sick.

- **Er hat Fieber.** (pronounced: air haht fee-ber) – He has a fever.

- **Sie nimmt eine Tablette.** (pronounced: zee nimt eye-neh tah-ble-teh) – She takes a pill.

- **Der Husten ist stark.** (pronounced: dair hoo-sten ist shtark) – The cough is strong.

These sentences show how to use health-related vocabulary to talk about common illnesses and symptoms.

Talking About Symptoms and Conditions

When you are not feeling well, it is important to be able to describe your symptoms. Here are some common phrases in German to help you do that:

- **Ich habe Kopfschmerzen.** (pronounced: ikh hah-beh kopf-shmairt-sen) – I have a headache.

- **Mein Bauch tut weh.** (pronounced: mine bowkh toot vay) – My stomach hurts.

- **Ich habe Halsschmerzen.** (pronounced: ikh hah-beh hals-shmairt-sen) – I have a sore throat.

- **Meine Augen sind rot.** (pronounced: my-neh ow-gen zind roht) – My eyes are red.

- **Mir ist übel.** (pronounced: meer ist oo-bel) – I feel nauseous.

These phrases will help you explain how you feel and describe your symptoms to someone, like a doctor or a friend.

Visiting the Doctor

If you need to visit a doctor, here are some useful words and phrases in German:

- **der Arzt** (pronounced: dair artz) – doctor (male)
- **die Ärztin** (pronounced: dee air-ts-tin) – doctor (female)
- **die Praxis** (pronounced: dee prahk-sis) – doctor's office
- **der Termin** (pronounced: dair ter-meen) – appointment
- **die Apotheke** (pronounced: dee ah-poh-tay-keh) – pharmacy
- **das Rezept** (pronounced: das re-tsept) – prescription
- **die Untersuchung** (pronounced: dee oon-ter-zoo-koong) – examination

Here are some sentences using these words:

- **Ich habe einen Termin beim Arzt.** (pronounced: ikh hah-beh eye-nen ter-meen bym arts) – I have an appointment with the doctor.
- **Sie geht zur Apotheke.** (pronounced: zee geht tsoor ah-poh-tay-keh) – She is going to the pharmacy.
- **Der Arzt gibt mir ein Rezept.** (pronounced: dair artz gibt meer ayn re-tsept) – The doctor gives me a prescription.
- **Er braucht eine Untersuchung.** (pronounced: air brow-kht eye-neh oon-ter-zoo-koong) – He needs an examination.

These phrases will help you when visiting a doctor or picking up medicine at a pharmacy.

Staying Healthy

Staying healthy is important. Here are some phrases that can help you talk about good habits and staying well in German:

- **Ich esse gesund.** (pronounced: ikh es-seh geh-zund) – I eat healthy.
- **Ich trinke viel Wasser.** (pronounced: ikh trin-keh feel vahs-ser) – I drink a lot of water.
- **Ich mache Sport.** (pronounced: ikh mah-kheh shport) – I do sports.

- **Ich schlafe genug.** (pronounced: ikh shlah-feh geh-nook) – I sleep enough.

- **Ich gehe regelmäßig spazieren.** (pronounced: ikh geh-heh ray-gel-mah-sig shpah-tseer-ren) – I go for regular walks.

These phrases help you describe good habits for staying healthy.

Key Points to Remember

- **Body Parts:** Learn the names of body parts like "Kopf" (head) and "Hand" (hand) to describe where you feel pain.

- **Health Terms:** Know words like "krank" (sick) and "gesund" (healthy) to talk about your health.

- **Describing Symptoms:** Use phrases like "Ich habe Kopfschmerzen" to explain your symptoms.

- **Visiting the Doctor:** Understand terms like "Arzt" (doctor) and "Termin" (appointment) for medical visits.

- **Healthy Habits:** Learn phrases that describe good habits, such as "Ich esse gesund" (I eat healthy).

Chapter 24

Jobs and Professions

Knowing how to talk about different jobs and professions is very useful in any language. Whether you're asking someone about their job, saying what you want to be when you grow up, or just describing people around you, it's important to have the right words. In this chapter, we will learn the German vocabulary for common jobs and professions. Let's start with some basic terms!

Common Jobs and Professions in German

Here are some common German words for different jobs and professions:

- **der Lehrer / die Lehrerin** (pronounced: dair lay-rer / dee lay-reh-rin) – male teacher / female teacher

- **der Arzt / die Ärztin** (pronounced: dair arts / dee air-ts-tin) – male doctor / female doctor

- **der Ingenieur / die Ingenieurin** (pronounced: dair in-jeh-nyoer / dee in-jeh-nyoer-in) – male engineer / female engineer

- **der Polizist / die Polizistin** (pronounced: dair poh-lee-tsist / dee poh-lee-tsis-tin) – male police officer / female police officer

- **der Verkäufer / die Verkäuferin** (pronounced: dair fer-koy-fer / dee fer-koy-feh-rin) – male salesperson / female salesperson

- **der Koch / die Köchin** (pronounced: dair kohkh / dee kuh-khin) – male cook / female cook

- **der Architekt / die Architektin** (pronounced: dair ar-khi-tekt / dee ar-khi-tek-tin) – male architect / female architect

- **der Journalist / die Journalistin** (pronounced: dair yohr-nah-list / dee yohr-nah-lis-tin) – male journalist / female journalist

- **der Künstler / die Künstlerin** (pronounced: dair kuenst-ler / dee kuenst-leh-rin) – male artist / female artist

- **der Anwalt / die Anwältin** (pronounced: dair ahn-vahlt / dee ahn-velt-in) – male lawyer / female lawyer

These words will help you talk about different professions in German. Let's see how to use them in sentences.

Using Profession Words in Sentences

Here are some examples of how to use these profession words in sentences:

- **Meine Mutter ist Lehrerin.** (pronounced: my-neh moo-ter ist lay-reh-rin) – My mother is a teacher.

- **Er ist Arzt und arbeitet im Krankenhaus.** (pronounced: air ist arts oont ar-bai-tet im krang-en-howz) – He is a doctor and works in a hospital.

- **Sie ist Ingenieurin und liebt ihren Beruf.** (pronounced: zee ist in-jeh-nyoer-in oont leebt ee-ren be-roof) – She is an engineer and loves her job.

- **Mein Vater ist Polizist.** (pronounced: mine fah-ter ist poh-lee-tsist) – My father is a police officer.

These sentences show how you can talk about what people do for work and where they work.

Describing What People Do at Their Jobs

It's also helpful to know how to describe what people do at their jobs. Here are some phrases that can help:

- **Er unterrichtet Schüler.** (pronounced: air oon-ter-rikh-tet shoo-ler) – He teaches students.

- **Sie untersucht Patienten.** (pronounced: zee oon-ter-zookht pa-tsee-en-ten) – She examines patients.

- **Er plant Gebäude.** (pronounced: air plahnt geh-boy-deh) – He designs buildings.

- **Sie schreibt Artikel.** (pronounced: zee shribt ar-tee-kel) – She writes articles.

These sentences help you explain what different professionals do in their jobs.

Talking About Future Jobs

Many people like to talk about what they want to be when they grow up. Here are some ways to say that in German:

- **Ich möchte Arzt werden.** (pronounced: ikh merkh-teh arts vair-den) – I want to become a doctor.

- **Er will Ingenieur werden.** (pronounced: air vil in-jeh-nyoer vair-den) – He wants to become an engineer.

- **Sie möchte Lehrerin werden.** (pronounced: zee merkh-teh lay-reh-rin vair-den) – She wants to become a teacher.

- **Wir möchten Künstler werden.** (pronounced: veer merkh-ten kuenst-ler vair-den) – We want to become artists.

These phrases will help you talk about future aspirations and dreams for different jobs.

Workplaces in German

It's also useful to know the German words for different places where people work:

- **das Büro** (pronounced: das byoo-roh) – office

- **das Krankenhaus** (pronounced: das krang-en-howz) – hospital

- **die Schule** (pronounced: dee shoo-leh) – school

- **die Werkstatt** (pronounced: dee verk-shtat) – workshop

- **das Geschäft** (pronounced: das ge-shaft) – store, shop

- **die Fabrik** (pronounced: dee fa-brik) – factory

- **das Restaurant** (pronounced: das re-sto-rahnt) – restaurant

Knowing these words will help you describe where people work. Here are some examples:

- **Er arbeitet im Büro.** (pronounced: air ar-bai-tet im byoo-roh) – He works in an office.

- **Sie arbeitet im Krankenhaus.** (pronounced: zee ar-bai-tet im krang-en-howz) – She works in a hospital.

- **Meine Mutter arbeitet in einer Schule.** (pronounced: my-neh moo-ter ar-bai-tet in eye-ner shoo-leh) – My mother works in a school.

- **Mein Vater arbeitet in einer Fabrik.** (pronounced: mine fah-ter ar-bai-tet in eye-ner fa-brik) – My father works in a factory.

These sentences will help you describe where someone works and what they do there.

Talking About Different Jobs

There are many different types of jobs people can have. Here are a few more professions in German:

- **der Mechaniker / die Mechanikerin** (pronounced: dair meh-kha-ni-ker / dee meh-kha-ni-ke-rin) – male mechanic / female mechanic

- **der Fahrer / die Fahrerin** (pronounced: dair fah-rer / dee fah-reh-rin) – male driver / female driver

- **der Bäcker / die Bäckerin** (pronounced: dair bek-er / dee bek-er-in) – male baker / female baker

- **der Musiker / die Musikerin** (pronounced: dair moo-zee-ker / dee moo-zee-ke-rin) – male musician / female musician

Here are some examples to help you use these words:

- **Er ist Mechaniker und repariert Autos.** (pronounced: air ist meh-kha-ni-ker oont re-pa-reet ow-tos) – He is a mechanic and repairs cars.

- **Sie ist Musikerin und spielt Klavier.** (pronounced: zee ist moo-zee-ke-rin oont shpeelt kla-veer) – She is a musician and plays the piano.

These examples show how to use different job titles in sentences.

Key Points to Remember

- **Common Professions:** Learn words like "Lehrer" (teacher) and "Arzt" (doctor) to talk about different jobs.

- **Describing Jobs:** Use phrases like "Er unterrichtet Schüler" to describe what people do in their jobs.

- **Future Jobs:** Talk about future careers using phrases like "Ich möchte Arzt werden."

- **Workplaces:** Learn the names of places people work, like "Büro" (office) and "Krankenhaus" (hospital).

- **Different Jobs:** Use job titles like "Mechaniker" (mechanic) and "Musiker" (musician) to describe various professions.

Chapter 25

Education and School Vocabulary

Learning about school and education vocabulary is important, especially if you are a student or want to talk about school-related topics in German. In this chapter, we will cover the basic German words related to school, different subjects, people you meet at school, and common phrases you might use in a classroom. Let's begin with some essential words!

Basic School Words in German

Here are some common German words you will hear when talking about school:

- **die Schule** (pronounced: dee shoo-leh) – school

- **das Klassenzimmer** (pronounced: das klas-sen-tsim-mer) – classroom

- **der Lehrer / die Lehrerin** (pronounced: dair lay-rer / dee lay-reh-rin) – male teacher / female teacher

- **der Schüler / die Schülerin** (pronounced: dair shoo-ler / dee shoo-leh-rin) – male student / female student

- **das Fach** (pronounced: das fahkh) – subject

- **die Pause** (pronounced: dee pow-zeh) – break, recess

- **die Hausaufgabe** (pronounced: dee hows-owf-gah-beh) – homework

- **die Prüfung** (pronounced: dee prue-foong) – exam, test

- **das Buch** (pronounced: das bookh) – book

- **der Schreibtisch** (pronounced: dair shribe-tish) – desk

These words will help you talk about different things related to school. Let's see how to use them in sentences.

Using School Words in Sentences

Here are some examples of how to use these school-related words in sentences:

- **Ich gehe zur Schule.** (pronounced: ikh geh-heh tsoor shoo-leh) – I go to school.

- **Das Klassenzimmer ist groß.** (pronounced: das klas-sen-tsim-mer ist gross) – The classroom is big.

- **Der Lehrer erklärt die Aufgabe.** (pronounced: dair lay-rer ek-lairt dee owf-gah-beh) – The teacher explains the task.

- **Die Schüler machen ihre Hausaufgaben.** (pronounced: dee shoo-ler mah-khen ee-reh hows-owf-gah-ben) – The students are doing their homework.

These sentences show how you can talk about different activities and things in a school setting.

Subjects in School

It is also important to know the German names for different school subjects. Here are some common ones:

- **Mathematik** (pronounced: mah-teh-mah-teek) – mathematics

- **Englisch** (pronounced: eng-lish) – English

- **Deutsch** (pronounced: doytch) – German

- **Biologie** (pronounced: bee-oh-loh-gee-eh) – biology

- **Geschichte** (pronounced: geh-shikh-teh) – history

- **Kunst** (pronounced: koonst) – art

- **Musik** (pronounced: moo-zeek) – music

- **Sport** (pronounced: shport) – physical education (PE)

- **Physik** (pronounced: fue-zeek) – physics

- **Chemie** (pronounced: ke-mee-eh) – chemistry

These words will help you talk about what subjects you are studying or what classes you have in school.

Using Subject Words in Sentences

Here are some examples of how to use these words in sentences:

- **Ich habe heute Mathematik.** (pronounced: ikh hah-beh hoy-teh mah-teh-mah-teek) – I have math today.

- **Wir lernen Englisch und Deutsch.** (pronounced: veer lair-nen eng-lish oont doytch) – We learn English and German.

- **Sie mag Kunst und Musik.** (pronounced: zee mahg koonst oont moo-zeek) – She likes art and music.

- **Biologie ist sehr interessant.** (pronounced: bee-oh-loh-gee-eh ist zair in-teh-re-sant) – Biology is very interesting.

These sentences help you talk about your favorite subjects or what you are studying.

People in School

There are many people you meet at school, such as teachers, students, and others who work there. Here are some common German words for people you might find in a school:

- **der Direktor / die Direktorin** (pronounced: dair dee-rek-tor / dee dee-rek-to-rin) – male principal / female principal

- **der Lehrer / die Lehrerin** (pronounced: dair lay-rer / dee lay-reh-rin) – male teacher / female teacher

- **der Schüler / die Schülerin** (pronounced: dair shoo-ler / dee shoo-leh-rin) – male student / female student

- **der Hausmeister** (pronounced: dair hows-my-ster) – male janitor

- **die Sekretärin** (pronounced: dee zek-re-tair-in) – female secretary

- **der Schulberater / die Schulberaterin** (pronounced: dair shool-beh-rah-ter / dee shool-beh-rah-te-rin) – male counselor / female counselor

These words will help you identify the different people you see in a school setting. Here are some sentences using these words:

- **Der Direktor spricht mit den Lehrern.** (pronounced: dair dee-rek-tor shprikht mit den lay-rern) – The principal is speaking with the teachers.

- **Die Sekretärin arbeitet im Büro.** (pronounced: dee zek-re-tair-in ar-bai-tet im byoo-roh) – The secretary works in the office.

- **Der Hausmeister repariert das Klassenzimmer.** (pronounced: dair hows-my-ster reh-pah-reet das klas-sen-tsim-mer) – The janitor repairs the classroom.

These examples help you understand who does what in a school environment.

Common School Phrases

Here are some useful phrases that you might hear or use in a school setting:

- **Wie heißt das auf Deutsch?** (pronounced: vee heist das owf doytch) – What is that called in German?

- **Können Sie das wiederholen?** (pronounced: koe-nen zee das vee-der-hoh-len) – Can you repeat that?

- **Ich habe meine Hausaufgaben gemacht.** (pronounced: ikh hah-beh my-neh hows-owf-gah-ben geh-mahkt) – I did my homework.

- **Wann ist die Pause?** (pronounced: vahn ist dee pow-zeh) – When is the break?

- **Was lernen wir heute?** (pronounced: vahs lair-nen veer hoy-teh) – What are we learning today?

These phrases will help you communicate effectively in a German classroom.

Talking About Your School Day

It is also helpful to know how to talk about your school day. Here are some examples:

- **Meine Schule beginnt um acht Uhr.** (pronounced: my-neh shoo-leh beh-gint oom ahkht oo-er) – My school starts at 8 o'clock.

- **Ich habe drei Stunden Englisch.** (pronounced: ikh hah-beh dry shtoon-den eng-lish) – I have three hours of English.

- **Wir haben eine lange Pause um zwölf Uhr.** (pronounced: veer hah-ben eye-neh lahng-geh pow-zeh oom tsvolf oo-er) – We have a long break at 12 o'clock.

- **Nach der Schule gehe ich nach Hause.** (pronounced: nahkh dair shoo-leh geh-heh ikh nahkh how-zeh) – After school, I go home.

These sentences help you describe your daily school routine.

Key Points to Remember

- **Basic School Words:** Learn words like "Schule" (school) and "Klassenzimmer" (classroom) to talk about school-related topics.

- **School Subjects:** Know the names of subjects like "Mathematik" (math) and "Biologie" (biology).

- **People in School:** Understand words like "Lehrer" (teacher) and "Schüler" (student) to talk about people at school.

- **Common Phrases:** Use phrases like "Können Sie das wiederholen?" to communicate in a classroom setting.

- **Daily School Routine:** Learn how to describe your school day with phrases like "Meine Schule beginnt um acht Uhr."

Chapter 26

Entertainment and Leisure Activities

Having fun and relaxing during your free time is an important part of life. Entertainment and leisure activities help you unwind, explore new interests, and spend time with friends and family. In this chapter, we will learn some useful German vocabulary for different types of entertainment and leisure activities. You will learn how to talk about your hobbies, favorite activities, and how to ask others about what they like to do for fun. Let's get started!

Common Leisure Activities

Here are some common German words for leisure activities you might enjoy:

- **lesen** (pronounced: lay-zen) – to read

- **fernsehen** (pronounced: fayrn-zay-en) – to watch TV

- **ins Kino gehen** (pronounced: ins kee-noh geh-en) – to go to the movies

- **Musik hören** (pronounced: moo-zeek hur-ren) – to listen to music

- **Computerspiele spielen** (pronounced: kom-pyoo-ter-shpee-leh shpee-len) – to play computer games

- **mit Freunden abhängen** (pronounced: mit froyn-den ahb-hen-gen) – to hang out with friends

- **Sport treiben** (pronounced: shport try-ben) – to play sports

- **im Internet surfen** (pronounced: im in-ter-net ser-fen) – to surf the internet

These words will help you talk about the activities you like to do in your free time. Let's see how to use them in sentences.

Using Leisure Activity Words in Sentences

Here are some examples of how to use these words in sentences:

- **Ich lese gerne Bücher.** (pronounced: ikh lay-zeh gair-neh boo-kher) – I like to read books.

- **Er sieht jeden Abend fern.** (pronounced: air zeet yay-den ah-bent fayrn) – He watches TV every evening.

- **Wir gehen am Wochenende ins Kino.** (pronounced: veer geh-en ahm vokh-en-en-deh ins kee-noh) – We go to the movies on the weekend.

- **Sie hört Musik, wenn sie Hausaufgaben macht.** (pronounced: zee hurt moo-zeek ven zee hows-owf-gah-ben makht) – She listens to music when she does her homework.

These sentences show how you can talk about the activities you enjoy in your free time.

Talking About Your Hobbies

Everyone has hobbies that they enjoy. Here are some common hobbies and how to say them in German:

- **zeichnen** (pronounced: tsai-kh-nen) – to draw

- **malen** (pronounced: mah-len) – to paint

- **tanzen** (pronounced: tahn-tsen) – to dance

- **fotografieren** (pronounced: foh-toh-grah-fear-ren) – to take photos

- **kochen** (pronounced: koh-khen) – to cook

- **backen** (pronounced: bahk-ken) – to bake

- **reisen** (pronounced: rye-zen) – to travel

- **wandern** (pronounced: vahn-dern) – to hike

Let's use these words in sentences:

- **Ich zeichne gerne in meiner Freizeit.** (pronounced: ikh tsai-kh-neh gair-neh in my-ner fry-tsite) – I like to draw in my free time.

- **Er malt wunderschöne Bilder.** (pronounced: air mahlt voon-der-shur-neh bil-der) – He paints beautiful pictures.

- **Wir tanzen jeden Samstagabend.** (pronounced: veer tahn-tsen yay-den zams-tahg ah-bent) – We dance every Saturday evening.

- **Sie fotografiert gerne Landschaften.** (pronounced: zee foh-toh-grah-feert gair-neh lahnt-shaften) – She likes to photograph landscapes.

These sentences help you talk about your hobbies and interests.

Entertainment Options

There are many different ways to entertain yourself. Here are some common German words for different forms of entertainment:

- **das Kino** (pronounced: das kee-noh) – movie theater, cinema
- **das Theater** (pronounced: das teh-ah-ter) – theater
- **das Konzert** (pronounced: das kon-tsert) – concert
- **das Museum** (pronounced: das moo-zay-oom) – museum
- **der Freizeitpark** (pronounced: dair fry-tsite-park) – amusement park
- **der Zoo** (pronounced: dair tsoh) – zoo
- **die Bibliothek** (pronounced: dee bee-blee-oh-take) – library

Here are some examples of how to use these words in sentences:

- **Wir gehen morgen ins Kino.** (pronounced: veer geh-en mor-gen ins kee-noh) – We are going to the movies tomorrow.

- **Er liebt es, ins Theater zu gehen.** (pronounced: air leebt es ins teh-ah-ter tsoo geh-en) – He loves going to the theater.

- **Am Wochenende besuchen wir ein Museum.** (pronounced: ahm vokh-en-en-deh beh-zoo-khen veer ayn moo-zay-oom) – On the weekend, we visit a museum.

- **Die Kinder haben im Freizeitpark viel Spaß.** (pronounced: dee kin-der hah-ben im fry-tsite-park feel shpahs) – The children have a lot of fun at the amusement park.

These sentences will help you talk about where you like to go for entertainment.

Talking About Free Time

It's also important to know how to talk about your free time and what you like to do. Here are some useful phrases:

- **In meiner Freizeit lese ich gerne.** (pronounced: in my-ner fry-tsite lay-zeh ikh gair-neh) – In my free time, I like to read.

- **Was machst du am Wochenende?** (pronounced: vahs makhst doo ahm vokh-en-en-deh) – What do you do on the weekend?

- **Er spielt gerne Computerspiele.** (pronounced: air shpeelt gair-neh kom-pyoo-ter-shpee-leh) – He likes to play computer games.

- **Wir gehen oft ins Kino.** (pronounced: veer geh-en oft ins kee-noh) – We often go to the movies.

- **Sie hört Musik, wenn sie entspannt.** (pronounced: zee hurt moo-zeek ven zee ent-shpant) – She listens to music when she relaxes.

These phrases help you describe how you spend your free time and ask others about their activities.

Talking About Preferences

Knowing how to express your likes and dislikes is also important. Here are some phrases to help you talk about your preferences in German:

- **Ich mag Fußball.** (pronounced: ikh mahg foos-ball) – I like soccer.

- **Er mag es nicht, zu schwimmen.** (pronounced: air mahg es nikht tsoo shvim-men) – He doesn't like to swim.

- **Wir mögen Kunst und Musik.** (pronounced: veer mer-ghen koonst oont moo-zeek) – We like art and music.

- **Sie mag Theaterstücke.** (pronounced: zee mahg teh-ah-ter-shtuek-eh) – She likes plays.

- **Ich mag keine Horrorfilme.** (pronounced: ikh mahg kye-neh hor-ror-fil-meh) – I don't like horror movies.

These phrases will help you share what you like and don't like with others.

Asking Others About Their Interests

It's also fun to ask others about what they like to do. Here are some questions you can use to ask about someone's interests in German:

- **Was machst du gerne in deiner Freizeit?** (pronounced: vahs makhst doo gair-neh in dy-ner fry-tsite) – What do you like to do in your free time?

- **Welche Hobbys hast du?** (pronounced: vel-khe hob-bees hast doo) – What hobbies do you have?

- **Gehst du gerne ins Kino?** (pronounced: gehst doo gair-neh ins kee-noh) – Do you like going to the movies?

- **Magst du Sport?** (pronounced: mahgst doo shport) – Do you like sports?

- **Spielst du ein Instrument?** (pronounced: shpeelst doo ayn in-stroo-ment) – Do you play an instrument?

These questions can help you start a conversation about hobbies and interests with your friends.

Key Points to Remember

- **Leisure Activities:** Learn words like "lesen" (to read) and "Musik hören" (to listen to music) to talk about what you enjoy doing in your free time.

- **Hobbies:** Use words like "zeichnen" (to draw) and "tanzen" (to dance) to describe your hobbies.

- **Entertainment Options:** Know places like "Kino" (movie theater) and "Museum" (museum) for fun activities.

- **Preferences:** Use phrases like "Ich mag Fußball" to express what you like and don't like.

- **Asking About Interests:** Ask questions like "Was machst du gerne in deiner Freizeit?" to learn about others' hobbies and interests.

Chapter 27

Sports and Hobbies

Sports and hobbies are a great way to stay active, have fun, and learn new skills. Whether you enjoy playing team sports, individual sports, or spending time on a favorite hobby, it's important to know how to talk about these activities in German. In this chapter, we will learn the vocabulary for different sports and hobbies, and how to use these words in sentences. Let's dive in!

Common Sports in German

Here are some common German words for different sports:

- **Fußball** (pronounced: foos-ball) – soccer
- **Basketball** (pronounced: bas-ket-ball) – basketball
- **Volleyball** (pronounced: vol-ley-ball) – volleyball
- **Tennis** (pronounced: ten-nis) – tennis
- **Schwimmen** (pronounced: shvim-men) – swimming
- **Laufen** (pronounced: low-fen) – running
- **Radfahren** (pronounced: rahd-fah-ren) – cycling
- **Turnen** (pronounced: toor-nen) – gymnastics
- **Reiten** (pronounced: rye-ten) – horseback riding
- **Eislaufen** (pronounced: ice-low-fen) – ice skating

These words will help you talk about the sports you enjoy or would like to try. Let's see how to use them in sentences.

Using Sports Words in Sentences

Here are some examples of how to use these sports words in sentences:

- **Ich spiele gern Fußball.** (pronounced: ikh shpee-leh gairn foos-ball) – I like to play soccer.

- **Er spielt Basketball in seiner Freizeit.** (pronounced: air shpeelt bas-ket-ball in zy-ner fry-tsite) – He plays basketball in his free time.

- **Wir schwimmen jeden Samstag im Schwimmbad.** (pronounced: veer shvim-men yay-den zams-tahg im shvim-bahd) – We swim every Saturday at the swimming pool.

- **Sie fährt gern Rad im Park.** (pronounced: zee fehrt gairn rahd im park) – She likes to ride a bike in the park.

These sentences help you talk about the sports you play or enjoy watching.

Talking About Hobbies

Hobbies are activities you do for fun, relaxation, or learning. Here are some common German words for different hobbies:

- **Fotografieren** (pronounced: foh-toh-grah-fear-ren) – photography

- **Malen** (pronounced: mah-len) – painting

- **Zeichnen** (pronounced: tsai-kh-nen) – drawing

- **Musik machen** (pronounced: moo-zeek mah-khen) – making music

- **Tanzen** (pronounced: tahn-tsen) – dancing

- **Gärtnern** (pronounced: gairt-nern) – gardening

- **Kochen** (pronounced: koh-khen) – cooking

- **Basteln** (pronounced: bas-teln) – crafting

Let's use these words in sentences to describe different hobbies:

- **Ich fotografiere gerne die Natur.** (pronounced: ikh foh-toh-grah-fee-reh gair-neh dee nah-toor) – I like to photograph nature.

- **Sie malt bunte Bilder.** (pronounced: zee mahlt boon-teh bil-der) – She paints colorful pictures.

- **Er macht gerne Musik auf der Gitarre.** (pronounced: air mahkt gair-neh moo-zeek owf dair gee-tar-reh) – He likes to make music on the guitar.

- **Wir tanzen zusammen im Tanzkurs.** (pronounced: veer tahn-tsen tsoo-zahm-men im tahnz-koors) – We dance together in the dance class.

These sentences show how to describe what hobbies you enjoy doing.

Expressing What You Like or Dislike

It's important to know how to say what you like or dislike in German. Here are some phrases to help you express your preferences:

- **Ich mag Basketball, aber ich mag kein Tennis.** (pronounced: ikh mahg bas-ket-ball, ah-ber ikh mahg kine ten-nis) – I like basketball, but I don't like tennis.

- **Er liebt es, zu schwimmen.** (pronounced: air leebt es tsoo shvim-men) – He loves swimming.

- **Sie mag kein Fußball spielen.** (pronounced: zee mahg kine foos-ball shpee-len) – She does not like playing soccer.

- **Wir mögen verschiedene Sportarten.** (pronounced: veer mer-ghen fer-shi-e-de-ne shport-ar-ten) – We like different sports.

These phrases help you talk about your favorite sports and hobbies and share your interests with others.

Talking About Sports Teams and Events

It can also be fun to talk about sports teams, events, and competitions. Here are some useful German words and phrases:

- **die Mannschaft** (pronounced: dee man-shaft) – team

- **das Spiel** (pronounced: das shpeel) – game, match

- **das Turnier** (pronounced: das toor-neer) – tournament

- **der Wettkampf** (pronounced: dair vet-kampf) – competition

- **gewinnen** (pronounced: geh-vin-nen) – to win
- **verlieren** (pronounced: fer-lee-ren) – to lose

Here are some sentences using these words:

- **Unsere Mannschaft hat das Spiel gewonnen.** (pronounced: oon-ze-re man-shaft haht das shpeel geh-von-nen) – Our team won the game.
- **Er spielt im nächsten Turnier.** (pronounced: air shpeelt im naekhs-ten toor-neer) – He is playing in the next tournament.
- **Sie haben den Wettkampf verloren.** (pronounced: zee hah-ben den vet-kampf fer-loh-ren) – They lost the competition.

These phrases help you talk about sports events and how your team is doing in a competition.

How to Ask About Hobbies and Sports

To start a conversation, you might want to ask someone about their hobbies or sports interests. Here are some useful questions:

- **Was ist dein Lieblingssport?** (pronounced: vahs ist dine leeb-lings-shport) – What is your favorite sport?
- **Welche Hobbys hast du?** (pronounced: vel-khe hob-bees hast doo) – What hobbies do you have?
- **Spielst du in einer Mannschaft?** (pronounced: shpeelst doo in eye-ner man-shaft) – Do you play on a team?
- **Magst du es, Tennis zu spielen?** (pronounced: mahgst doo es ten-nis tsoo shpee-len) – Do you like to play tennis?

These questions can help you learn more about what sports and hobbies others enjoy.

Key Points to Remember

- **Common Sports:** Learn words like "Fußball" (soccer) and "Schwimmen" (swimming) to talk about sports you enjoy.
- **Hobbies:** Use words like "Fotografieren" (photography) and "Zeichnen" (drawing) to describe your hobbies.

- **Expressing Preferences:** Use phrases like "Ich mag Basketball" to share what you like or dislike.

- **Talking About Events:** Know words like "Mannschaft" (team) and "Spiel" (game) to discuss sports events.

- **Asking About Interests:** Use questions like "Was ist dein Lieblingssport?" to ask others about their favorite sports.

Chapter 28

Nature and Environment

The natural world around us is full of beauty and wonder. Learning how to talk about nature and the environment in German can help you describe the world you see every day, whether you are talking about the weather, plants, animals, or different landscapes. In this chapter, we will learn some basic German vocabulary related to nature and the environment. Let's explore these words together!

Basic Words for Nature

Let's start with some common German words related to nature:

- **die Natur** (pronounced: dee nah-toor) – nature
- **der Baum** (pronounced: dair bowm) – tree
- **die Blume** (pronounced: dee bloo-meh) – flower
- **das Gras** (pronounced: das grahs) – grass
- **der Wald** (pronounced: dair vahlt) – forest
- **der Fluss** (pronounced: dair floos) – river
- **der Berg** (pronounced: dair bairg) – mountain
- **der Himmel** (pronounced: dair him-mel) – sky
- **das Meer** (pronounced: das mehr) – sea
- **der See** (pronounced: dair zay) – lake

These words will help you describe different parts of the natural world around you. Let's see how to use them in sentences.

Using Nature Words in Sentences

Here are some examples of how to use these nature words in sentences:

- **Die Blumen im Garten sind schön.** (pronounced: dee bloo-men im gart-en zind shern) – The flowers in the garden are beautiful.

- **Der Baum ist sehr groß.** (pronounced: dair bowm ist zair gross) – The tree is very big.

- **Wir wandern im Wald.** (pronounced: veer vahn-dern im vahlt) – We are hiking in the forest.

- **Das Meer ist heute ruhig.** (pronounced: das mehr ist hoy-teh roo-ikh) – The sea is calm today.

These sentences help you describe the natural world around you and talk about different features of nature.

Talking About Animals

Animals are an important part of nature. Here are some common German words for different animals:

- **der Hund** (pronounced: dair hoont) – dog

- **die Katze** (pronounced: dee kaht-zeh) – cat

- **der Vogel** (pronounced: dair fo-gel) – bird

- **die Biene** (pronounced: dee bee-neh) – bee

- **der Fisch** (pronounced: dair fish) – fish

- **das Pferd** (pronounced: das fehrt) – horse

- **der Löwe** (pronounced: dair luh-veh) – lion

- **der Elefant** (pronounced: dair eh-leh-fahnt) – elephant

- **der Frosch** (pronounced: dair frosh) – frog

- **der Schmetterling** (pronounced: dair shmet-ter-ling) – butterfly

Let's use these animal words in sentences:

- **Ich habe einen Hund und eine Katze.** (pronounced: ikh hah-beh eye-nen hoont oont eye-neh kaht-zeh) – I have a dog and a cat.

- **Der Vogel singt schön.** (pronounced: dair fo-gel singt shern) – The bird sings beautifully.

- **Die Biene fliegt von Blume zu Blume.** (pronounced: dee bee-neh fleegt fon bloo-meh tsoo bloo-meh) – The bee flies from flower to flower.

- **Der Elefant ist sehr groß.** (pronounced: dair eh-leh-fahnt ist zair gross) – The elephant is very big.

These sentences help you talk about different animals and describe what they do.

Weather and Seasons

Weather and seasons are important parts of the natural environment. Here are some useful German words for talking about weather and seasons:

- **das Wetter** (pronounced: das vet-ter) – weather

- **die Sonne** (pronounced: dee zon-neh) – sun

- **der Regen** (pronounced: dair ray-gen) – rain

- **der Schnee** (pronounced: dair shnay) – snow

- **der Wind** (pronounced: dair vint) – wind

- **der Frühling** (pronounced: dair froo-ling) – spring

- **der Sommer** (pronounced: dair zom-mer) – summer

- **der Herbst** (pronounced: dair hairpst) – autumn, fall

- **der Winter** (pronounced: dair vin-ter) – winter

Let's see how to use these words in sentences:

- **Das Wetter ist heute sonnig.** (pronounced: das vet-ter ist hoy-teh zon-nig) – The weather is sunny today.

- **Es regnet oft im Herbst.** (pronounced: es rayg-net oft im hairpst) – It often rains in the fall.

- **Im Winter schneit es.** (pronounced: im vin-ter shnite es) – It snows in the winter.

- **Der Frühling ist meine Lieblingsjahreszeit.** (pronounced: dair froo-ling ist my-neh leeb-lings-yah-res-tsite) – Spring is my favorite season.

These sentences help you talk about the weather and the different seasons of the year.

Environmental Conservation

Taking care of our environment is very important. Here are some German words related to environmental conservation:

- **der Umweltschutz** (pronounced: dair oom-velt-shoots) – environmental protection

- **das Recycling** (pronounced: das ree-sai-kling) – recycling

- **die Verschmutzung** (pronounced: dee fair-shmoot-soong) – pollution

- **die Natur schützen** (pronounced: dee nah-toor shoot-sen) – to protect nature

- **die erneuerbare Energie** (pronounced: dee er-noy-er-bar-eh eh-ner-ghee-eh) – renewable energy

- **der Abfall** (pronounced: dair ahb-fahl) – waste, trash

- **der Klimawandel** (pronounced: dair klee-mah-vahn-del) – climate change

Here are some sentences using these words:

- **Wir recyceln Papier und Plastik.** (pronounced: veer ree-sai-keln pah-peer oont plah-stick) – We recycle paper and plastic.

- **Umweltschutz ist wichtig für die Zukunft.** (pronounced: oom-velt-shoots ist vikh-tig foo-er dee tsoo-kunft) – Environmental protection is important for the future.

- **Der Klimawandel beeinflusst das Wetter.** (pronounced: dair klee-mah-vahn-del be-eye-nfloost das vet-ter) – Climate change affects the weather.

These sentences help you talk about actions to protect the environment and the importance of conservation.

Key Points to Remember

- **Nature Vocabulary:** Learn words like "Baum" (tree) and "Meer" (sea) to describe the natural world around you.

- **Animals:** Use words like "Hund" (dog) and "Schmetterling" (butterfly) to talk about different animals.

- **Weather and Seasons:** Know words like "Regen" (rain) and "Sommer" (summer) to discuss weather and seasons.

- **Conservation Terms:** Learn terms like "Umweltschutz" (environmental protection) and "Recycling" to talk about protecting the environment.

- **Describing the Environment:** Use these vocabulary words to describe different aspects of nature and our planet.

Chapter 29

Common Idioms and Expressions

Learning idioms and expressions is an important part of understanding any language. Idioms are phrases that have a special meaning that is different from the literal meaning of the words. Expressions are commonly used phrases that can help you sound more like a native speaker. In this chapter, we will explore some common German idioms and expressions, what they mean, and how to use them. Let's dive in and have some fun with the colorful language of idioms!

What Are Idioms?

Idioms are phrases where the meaning is different from the individual words. For example, in English, the phrase "it's raining cats and dogs" doesn't mean that cats and dogs are falling from the sky; it just means it's raining very heavily. Similarly, German has its own idioms that might sound funny or strange at first, but they are used often in everyday conversation.

Common German Idioms

Here are some popular German idioms, their meanings, and how to pronounce them:

- **Alles in Butter** (pronounced: ah-les in boot-ter) – Everything is fine.
  This idiom literally translates to "everything in butter," but it is used to mean that everything is going smoothly or is okay.
  Example: **Keine Sorge, alles in Butter!** (pronounced: ky-neh zor-guh, ah-les in boot-ter) – Don't worry, everything is fine!

- **Tomaten auf den Augen haben** (pronounced: toh-mah-ten owf den ow-gen hah-ben) – To be oblivious to what is happening around you.
  This literally means "to have tomatoes on your eyes." It is used when someone is not seeing something obvious or is missing something right in front of them.
  Example: **Hast du Tomaten auf den Augen?** (pronounced: hahst doo toh-mah-ten owf den ow-gen) – Are you not seeing what's obvious?

- **Da steppt der Bär** (pronounced: dah shtept dair bair) – There's a great party or event happening.
  This idiom literally translates to "there the bear dances," but it means that something exciting or fun is happening.
  Example: **Heute Abend steppt der Bär!** (pronounced: hoy-teh ah-bent shtept dair bair) – There will be a great party tonight!

- **Jemandem einen Bären aufbinden** (pronounced: yeh-mahn-dem eye-nen bair-en owf-bin-den) – To trick or fool someone.
  This idiom means "to tie a bear to someone," but it's used to say that you are telling someone a lie or fooling them.
  Example: **Er hat mir einen Bären aufgebunden.** (pronounced: air haht meer eye-nen bair-en owf-ge-boon-den) – He tricked me.

- **Das ist nicht mein Bier** (pronounced: das ist nikht mine beer) – That's not my problem or concern.
  This idiom translates to "that is not my beer," which means it is not something you are responsible for or involved in.
  Example: **Das ist nicht mein Bier.** (pronounced: das ist nikht mine beer) – That's not my concern.

Common German Expressions

Expressions are phrases that are used often in everyday speech. They help you sound more natural and fluent. Here are some common German expressions:

- **Auf Wiedersehen** (pronounced: owf vee-der-zay-en) – Goodbye.
  This is a common way to say goodbye in German. It literally means "until we see each other again."
  Example: **Auf Wiedersehen! Bis bald!** (pronounced: owf vee-der-zay-en! bis bahlt!) – Goodbye! See you soon!

- **Keine Sorge** (pronounced: ky-neh zor-guh) – Don't worry.
  This is used to reassure someone that everything is okay.
  Example: **Keine Sorge, ich helfe dir.** (pronounced: ky-neh zor-guh, ikh hel-feh deer) – Don't worry, I will help you.

- **Wie geht's?** (pronounced: vee gets?) – How are you?
  This is a common way to ask someone how they are doing.
  Example: **Hallo! Wie geht's dir heute?** (pronounced: hah-loh! vee gets deer hoy-teh?)

– Hello! How are you today?

- **Gute Besserung** (pronounced: goo-teh bes-se-roong) – Get well soon.
  This is a nice way to wish someone a speedy recovery if they are sick.
  Example: **Ich hoffe, du fühlst dich bald besser. Gute Besserung!** (pronounced: ikh hoh-feh, doo fyoolst dikh bahlt bes-ser. goo-teh bes-se-roong!) – I hope you feel better soon. Get well soon!

- **Bis später** (pronounced: bis shpay-ter) – See you later.
  This is a casual way to say goodbye, like saying "see you later" in English.
  Example: **Ich muss jetzt gehen. Bis später!** (pronounced: ikh moos yetst geh-en. bis shpay-ter!) – I have to go now. See you later!

Using Idioms and Expressions in Conversation

Using idioms and expressions can make your conversations more fun and interesting. They help you sound more natural and fluent when speaking in German. Here are some sentences that show how you might use these idioms and expressions in a conversation:

- **Freund 1:** Hallo! Wie geht's? (pronounced: hah-loh! vee gets?) – Hello! How are you?

- **Freund 2:** Alles in Butter! Und dir? (pronounced: ah-les in boot-ter! oont deer?) – Everything is fine! And you?

- **Freund 1:** Mir geht's gut. Ich habe gehört, dass heute Abend eine Party ist. (pronounced: meer gets goot. ikh hah-beh geh-hoert, dass hoy-teh ah-bent eye-neh par-tee ist) – I'm good. I heard there's a party tonight.

- **Freund 2:** Ja, da steppt der Bär! (pronounced: yah, dah shtept dair bair!) – Yes, it's going to be a great party!

This example shows how you can use both expressions and idioms to make your conversations more lively.

Why Idioms and Expressions Are Important

Learning idioms and expressions helps you understand the culture and humor of a language. They often reflect the way people think and express themselves. When you know idioms and expressions, you can better understand movies, songs, books, and everyday conversations in German. It also helps you connect more with native speakers and makes learning more enjoyable.

Key Points to Remember

- **Idioms Have Unique Meanings:** Remember that idioms do not mean what the individual words say; they have a special meaning, like "Tomaten auf den Augen haben" meaning "to be oblivious."

- **Expressions Are Everyday Phrases:** Learn expressions like "Auf Wiedersehen" to sound more like a native speaker.

- **Practice Using Idioms:** Try using idioms in your conversations to make them more fun and engaging.

- **Idioms Reflect Culture:** Understanding idioms helps you understand the culture and humor of the language better.

- **Keep Learning:** The more idioms and expressions you learn, the more natural your German will sound!

Chapter 30

Making Comparisons

When you want to talk about how two things are different or similar, you make comparisons. In English, you might say, "This apple is bigger than that apple" or "She runs faster than her brother." In German, we also use special words and forms to make comparisons. In this chapter, we will learn how to make comparisons in German using simple rules, words, and examples. Let's get started!

Basic Comparative Words

To make comparisons in German, you need to know some basic words. Here are a few key terms:

- **mehr** (pronounced: mehr) – more
- **weniger** (pronounced: veh-nee-ger) – less
- **als** (pronounced: als) – than
- **so ... wie** (pronounced: zoh ... vee) – as ... as

These words help you create basic comparisons in German. Let's look at how to use them in sentences.

Using Comparatives with Adjectives

In German, just like in English, you can change an adjective to make a comparison. Here's how it works:

To say that something is "bigger" or "smaller," we usually add "-er" to the end of the adjective:

- **groß** (pronounced: gross) – big
  größer (pronounced: grur-ser) – bigger

- **klein** (pronounced: kline) – small
  kleiner (pronounced: kline-er) – smaller

Let's see these adjectives in sentences:

- **Der Elefant ist größer als der Hund.** (pronounced: dair eh-le-fahnt ist grur-ser als dair hoont) – The elephant is bigger than the dog.
- **Der Ball ist kleiner als das Auto.** (pronounced: dair ball ist kline-er als das ow-toh) – The ball is smaller than the car.

You can use this pattern with many other adjectives to compare things in German.

Comparing Two Things: "More Than" and "Less Than"

To say that something has "more" or "less" of a quality than something else, we use the words **mehr** (more) and **weniger** (less), along with the word **als** (than). Here's how it works:

- **mehr ... als** (pronounced: mehr ... als) – more ... than
- **weniger ... als** (pronounced: veh-nee-ger ... als) – less ... than

Let's use these in sentences:

- **Ich habe mehr Bücher als du.** (pronounced: ikh hah-beh mehr boo-kher als doo) – I have more books than you.
- **Sie hat weniger Zeit als er.** (pronounced: zee haht veh-nee-ger tsight als air) – She has less time than he does.

These sentences show how you can compare two things by saying that one has more or less of something than the other.

Comparing Two Things That Are the Same

Sometimes, you might want to say that two things are the same in some way. In German, we use the phrase **so ... wie** (as ... as) to make these comparisons.

Here's how it works:

- **so groß wie** (pronounced: zoh gross vee) – as big as
- **so schnell wie** (pronounced: zoh shnell vee) – as fast as

Let's use these in sentences:

- **Der Apfel ist so groß wie die Orange.** (pronounced: dair ahp-fel ist zoh gross vee dee o-ran-ghe) – The apple is as big as the orange.

- **Er ist so schnell wie sein Bruder.** (pronounced: air ist zoh shnell vee zine broo-der) – He is as fast as his brother.

These sentences show how to express that two things are equal in some way.

Superlatives: The "Most" or "Least" of Something

When you want to say that something is the "most" or "least" of a certain quality, you use the superlative form. In German, we usually add "-ste" or "-este" to the adjective, and sometimes you use the word **am** before the adjective.

- **am größten** (pronounced: am grur-s-ten) – the biggest

- **am kleinsten** (pronounced: am kline-sten) – the smallest

Here are some examples in sentences:

- **Der Mount Everest ist der höchste Berg.** (pronounced: dair mownt eh-ver-est ist dair hoh-e-ste bairg) – Mount Everest is the highest mountain.

- **Der kleinste Hund ist im Haus.** (pronounced: dair kline-ste hoont ist im howss) – The smallest dog is in the house.

These sentences help you describe the most or least of something in German.

Tips for Making Comparisons

Here are a few tips to help you remember how to make comparisons in German:

- Remember that for most adjectives, you just add "-er" to make them comparative. For example, "schnell" (fast) becomes "schneller" (faster).

- Use "als" to say "than" when comparing two things: "größer als" (bigger than).

- Use "so ... wie" to say "as ... as" when comparing two things that are equal: "so groß wie" (as big as).

- For superlatives, add "-ste" or "-este" to say "the most" or "the least": "am größten" (the biggest), "am kleinsten" (the smallest).

Practice Making Comparisons

Try making some comparisons on your own! Here are a few ideas to get you started:

- Compare two animals: **Der Hund ist größer als die Katze.** (pronounced: dair hoont ist grur-ser als dee kaht-zeh) – The dog is bigger than the cat.

- Compare two objects: **Mein Buch ist dicker als dein Buch.** (pronounced: mine bookh ist dik-er als dine bookh) – My book is thicker than your book.

- Compare two people: **Meine Schwester ist so alt wie ich.** (pronounced: my-neh shvest-er ist zoh ahlt vee ikh) – My sister is as old as I am.

These examples will help you practice making comparisons in German, so you can describe things in more detail.

Key Points to Remember

- **Comparative Forms:** Add "-er" to adjectives to compare two things, like "größer" (bigger) and "kleiner" (smaller).

- **Using "More" and "Less":** Use "mehr" and "weniger" with "als" to say "more than" or "less than."

- **Equal Comparisons:** Use "so ... wie" to say two things are the same, like "so groß wie" (as big as).

- Superlatives: Add "-ste" or "-este" for superlatives, like "am größten" (the biggest).

- **Practice Comparing:** Use these forms to describe and compare things around you!

Chapter 31

Advanced Grammar: Subordinate Clauses

Subordinate clauses are an important part of German grammar. They help us connect ideas and provide more detail in sentences. In English, we use subordinate clauses when we say things like, "I will go to the park if it doesn't rain" or "She likes the book because it's interesting." In this chapter, we will learn what subordinate clauses are in German, how to use them, and some common words that introduce them. Let's start by understanding what a subordinate clause is!

What is a Subordinate Clause?

A subordinate clause is a part of a sentence that cannot stand alone as a complete sentence. It depends on the main clause to make sense. Subordinate clauses often start with words like "because," "if," "when," or "although." In German, subordinate clauses are also introduced by specific words, and they have a different word order than main clauses.

For example, in English, we might say:

I will go to the park if it doesn't rain.

In this sentence, "if it doesn't rain" is the subordinate clause. It gives more information about the main clause "I will go to the park."

Subordinate Clauses in German

In German, subordinate clauses are introduced by conjunctions (joining words) like **wenn** (if/when), **weil** (because), and **dass** (that). Here are some common German conjunctions that introduce subordinate clauses:

- **wenn** (pronounced: ven) – if, when

- **weil** (pronounced: vyle) – because

- **dass** (pronounced: dahs) – that

- **obwohl** (pronounced: ob-vohl) – although

- **während** (pronounced: vair-ent) – while

These words help introduce subordinate clauses in German sentences. Let's look at how to use them in sentences.

Word Order in Subordinate Clauses

One important thing to remember about subordinate clauses in German is that they have a different word order than main clauses. In a subordinate clause, the verb (the action word) comes at the end of the clause.

Here is a simple example:

- **Ich gehe zum Park, weil es nicht regnet.** (pronounced: ikh geh-heh tsoom park, vyle es nikht reg-net) – I am going to the park because it isn't raining.

In this sentence, the main clause is "Ich gehe zum Park" (I am going to the park), and the subordinate clause is "weil es nicht regnet" (because it isn't raining). Notice how in the subordinate clause, the verb "regnet" (is raining) comes at the end.

Here's another example:

- **Sie weiß, dass er heute kommt.** (pronounced: zee vise, dass air hoy-teh kommt) – She knows that he is coming today.

In this example, the main clause is "Sie weiß" (She knows), and the subordinate clause is "dass er heute kommt" (that he is coming today). The verb "kommt" (is coming) is at the end of the subordinate clause.

Examples of Subordinate Clauses with Common Conjunctions

Let's look at some more examples using common German conjunctions to make subordinate clauses:

- **Wenn** (if/when):
  Ich komme, wenn ich Zeit habe. (pronounced: ikh koh-meh, ven ikh tsight hah-beh) – I will come if I have time.

- **Weil** (because):
  Er bleibt zu Hause, weil er krank ist. (pronounced: air blybt tsoo how-zeh, vyle air krank ist) – He stays at home because he is sick.

- **Dass** (that):
  Sie sagt, dass sie morgen ankommt. (pronounced: zee zahkt, dass zee mor-gen an-kommt) – She says that she will arrive tomorrow.

- **Obwohl** (although):
  Ich gehe spazieren, obwohl es regnet. (pronounced: ikh geh-heh shpah-tsee-ren, ob-vohl es reg-net) – I go for a walk, although it is raining.

- **Während** (while):
  Wir essen, während wir fernsehen. (pronounced: veer ess-en, vair-ent veer fern-zay-en) – We eat while we watch TV.

These examples show how subordinate clauses are used with different conjunctions in German.

Combining Main Clauses and Subordinate Clauses

In German, subordinate clauses can come before or after the main clause. If the subordinate clause comes first, the main clause starts with the verb. Here are two examples:

- Subordinate Clause First: **Weil es regnet, gehe ich nicht nach draußen.** (pronounced: vyle es reg-net, geh-heh ikh nikht nahkh drow-sen) – Because it's raining, I am not going outside.

- Main Clause First: **Ich gehe nicht nach draußen, weil es regnet.** (pronounced: ikh geh-heh nikht nahkh drow-sen, vyle es reg-net) – I am not going outside because it's raining.

Notice how when the subordinate clause comes first, the verb in the main clause "gehe" (am going) comes directly after the comma.

Using Multiple Subordinate Clauses

Sometimes, sentences can have more than one subordinate clause to provide more details. Here's an example:

- **Ich weiß, dass du kommst, weil du mir geschrieben hast.** (pronounced: ikh vise, dass doo komst, vyle doo meer ge-shree-ben hahst) – I know that you are coming because you wrote to me.

In this sentence, there are two subordinate clauses: "dass du kommst" (that you are coming) and "weil du mir geschrieben hast" (because you wrote to me). This shows how German can connect multiple ideas within one sentence.

Tips for Using Subordinate Clauses

Here are some helpful tips to remember when using subordinate clauses in German:

- Always place the verb at the end of the subordinate clause.
- Remember to use a comma before the subordinate clause starts.
- If the subordinate clause comes first, the main clause starts with the verb.
- Use conjunctions like **wenn** (if/when), **weil** (because), and **dass** (that) to introduce subordinate clauses.
- Practice combining sentences to see how subordinate clauses work in real conversations.

Key Points to Remember

- **Subordinate Clauses:** These are parts of sentences that add extra information and start with words like "weil" (because) or "dass" (that).
- **Word Order:** The verb always comes at the end of a subordinate clause in German.
- **Combining Clauses:** You can use subordinate clauses before or after the main clause, but if they come first, the main clause starts with the verb.
- **Multiple Clauses:** Sentences can have more than one subordinate clause to connect different ideas.
- **Conjunctions Are Key:** Learn the common conjunctions like "wenn," "weil," and "dass" to start using subordinate clauses.

Chapter 32

Advanced Grammar: Passive Voice

In German, just like in English, we sometimes use the passive voice to focus on the action itself rather than who is doing the action. For example, instead of saying, "The dog eats the bone," in the active voice, we might say, "The bone is eaten by the dog" in the passive voice. In this chapter, we will learn how to form the passive voice in German and understand when to use it. Let's start with the basics!

What is Passive Voice?

The passive voice is a way of constructing a sentence so that the subject is the receiver of the action rather than the doer. In English, we use the passive voice when we say things like "The cake was baked by Maria." In this sentence, the cake (the subject) receives the action of being baked, rather than doing the action.

In German, we do the same thing with the help of the verb **werden** (pronounced: vair-den) combined with the past participle of the main verb. The verb **werden** changes according to the subject of the sentence.

How to Form the Passive Voice in German

To form the passive voice in German, you use the correct form of **werden** and the past participle of the main verb. Here's the basic formula:

Subject + form of "werden" + past participle of the verb

Let's look at an example:

- Active: **Der Lehrer erklärt die Regel.** (pronounced: dair lay-rer ek-lairt dee ray-gel) – The teacher explains the rule.

- Passive: **Die Regel wird vom Lehrer erklärt.** (pronounced: dee ray-gel vird fom lay-rer ek-lairt) – The rule is explained by the teacher.

In the passive sentence, **"wird"** is the form of **werden** that matches the subject "die Regel" (the rule), and "erklärt" is the past participle of the verb "erklären" (to explain).

Conjugating "Werden" in the Present Tense

To form the passive voice, you need to know how to conjugate **werden** in the present tense. Here is how it changes with different subjects:

- **ich werde** (pronounced: ikh vair-deh) – I become / I will
- **du wirst** (pronounced: doo virst) – you become / you will
- **er/sie/es wird** (pronounced: air/zee/es vird) – he/she/it becomes / he/she/it will
- **wir werden** (pronounced: veer vair-den) – we become / we will
- **ihr werdet** (pronounced: eer vair-det) – you (all) become / you (all) will
- **sie/Sie werden** (pronounced: zee/Zee vair-den) – they/you (formal) become / they/you (formal) will

These forms of **werden** are used to create the passive voice in the present tense.

Examples of Passive Voice in Present Tense

Let's look at some examples of how to use the passive voice in the present tense:

- **Die Tür wird geöffnet.** (pronounced: dee tur vird geh-oeff-net) – The door is being opened.
- **Das Essen wird gekocht.** (pronounced: das ess-en vird ge-kohkt) – The food is being cooked.
- **Der Brief wird geschrieben.** (pronounced: dair breef vird ge-shree-ben) – The letter is being written.
- **Die Bücher werden verkauft.** (pronounced: dee boo-kher vair-den fer-kowft) – The books are being sold.

In each of these examples, the action is being done to the subject, and the verb "werden" is used with the past participle to create the passive voice.

Passive Voice in the Past Tense

To form the passive voice in the past tense (also called the "simple past"), you use the correct form of **werden** in the past (which is **wurde**) and the past participle of the main verb. Here's the formula:

Subject + form of "wurde" + past participle of the verb

Here is how "werden" changes in the past tense:

- **ich wurde** (pronounced: ikh vur-deh) – I was
- **du wurdest** (pronounced: doo vur-dest) – you were
- **er/sie/es wurde** (pronounced: air/zee/es vur-deh) – he/she/it was
- **wir wurden** (pronounced: veer vur-den) – we were
- **ihr wurdet** (pronounced: eer vur-det) – you (all) were
- **sie/Sie wurden** (pronounced: zee/Zee vur-den) – they/you (formal) were

Examples of Passive Voice in Past Tense

Let's look at some examples of passive sentences in the past tense:

- **Das Auto wurde repariert.** (pronounced: das ow-toh vur-deh reh-pah-reet) – The car was repaired.
- **Der Kuchen wurde gebacken.** (pronounced: dair koo-khen vur-deh geh-bahk-en) – The cake was baked.
- **Die Nachrichten wurden gehört.** (pronounced: dee nah-khrikh-ten vur-den geh-hoert) – The news was heard.
- **Der Tisch wurde gedeckt.** (pronounced: dair tish vur-deh geh-deckt) – The table was set.

These examples show how the passive voice can be used to describe actions that happened in the past.

When to Use the Passive Voice

The passive voice is often used when the person doing the action is unknown, unimportant, or obvious from context. Here are some situations where you might use the passive voice:

- **When the focus is on the action:**
  Das Haus wird gebaut. (pronounced: das howss virt geh-bowt) – The house is being built.
  Here, the focus is on the building of the house, not on who is building it.

- **When the doer is not known:**
  Die Tasche wurde gefunden. (pronounced: dee tash-eh vur-deh ge-foon-den) – The bag was found.
  We don't know who found the bag, and it isn't important to the meaning of the sentence.

- **When the doer is obvious:**
  Das Essen wird serviert. (pronounced: das ess-en virt ser-veert) – The food is being served.
  It is clear that the waiter or chef is serving the food, so we don't need to mention it.

Using Passive Voice with Modal Verbs

Sometimes, you may need to use the passive voice with modal verbs (like "can," "must," or "should"). In German, you form this by using the modal verb with the infinitive **werden** and the past participle of the main verb:

- **Die Aufgabe muss gemacht werden.** (pronounced: dee owf-gah-beh moos geh-mahkt vair-den) – The task must be done.

- **Das Problem kann gelöst werden.** (pronounced: das prob-lem kahn geh-loest vair-den) – The problem can be solved.

These sentences show how you can combine the passive voice with modal verbs to express necessity or possibility.

Key Points to Remember

- **Passive Voice Formation:** Use "werden" plus the past participle of the main verb to form the passive voice.

- **Present Tense:** Use forms of "werden" like "wird" or "werden" with the past participle for present passive sentences.

- **Past Tense:** Use "wurde" or "wurden" with the past participle to form the passive in the past.

- **Use with Modals:** Combine modal verbs with the infinitive "werden" and the past participle for sentences like "must be done."

- **Purpose of Passive:** Use passive voice when the doer is unknown, unimportant, or obvious.

Chapter 33

Advanced Grammar: Reflexive Verbs

Reflexive verbs are an important part of German grammar. They are verbs where the action reflects back on the person who is doing it. This might sound confusing at first, but it's actually quite simple. In English, we use reflexive verbs when we say things like "I wash myself" or "She looks at herself in the mirror." In this chapter, we will learn what reflexive verbs are in German, how to use them, and which reflexive pronouns are needed. Let's start with the basics!

What Are Reflexive Verbs?

Reflexive verbs are verbs where the subject and the object of the sentence are the same. This means that the person doing the action is also receiving the action. For example, in the sentence "I wash myself," the person doing the washing is also the person being washed. In German, reflexive verbs use reflexive pronouns like "myself," "yourself," "himself," etc.

In German, reflexive verbs are often used with the reflexive pronoun **sich** (pronounced: zikh) for third-person forms or **mich** (myself), **dich** (yourself), and so on for other forms.

Reflexive Pronouns in German

To use reflexive verbs in German, you need to know the reflexive pronouns. Here is a list of reflexive pronouns in German:

- **ich** (I) – **mich** (myself) (pronounced: mikh)

- **du** (you, informal) – **dich** (yourself) (pronounced: dikh)

- **er/sie/es** (he/she/it) – **sich** (himself/herself/itself) (pronounced: zikh)

- **wir** (we) – **uns** (ourselves) (pronounced: oons)

- **ihr** (you all, informal) – **euch** (yourselves) (pronounced: oykh)

- **sie/Sie** (they/you, formal) – **sich** (themselves/yourself) (pronounced: zikh)

These pronouns are used with reflexive verbs to show that the action is being done to the subject itself. Let's see how to use them in sentences.

Using Reflexive Verbs in Sentences

Here are some examples of reflexive verbs in German and how they are used in sentences:

- **sich waschen** (to wash oneself) (pronounced: zikh vah-shen)
  Ich wasche mich. (pronounced: ikh vah-sheh mikh) – I wash myself.

- **sich anziehen** (to get dressed) (pronounced: zikh an-tsee-hen)
  Du ziehst dich an. (pronounced: doo tzeest dikh an) – You get dressed.

- **sich freuen** (to be happy) (pronounced: zikh froy-en)
  Er freut sich. (pronounced: air froy-t zikh) – He is happy.

- **sich setzen** (to sit down) (pronounced: zikh zet-sen)
  Wir setzen uns. (pronounced: veer zet-sen oons) – We sit down.

- **sich ausruhen** (to rest) (pronounced: zikh owss-roo-hen)
  Ihr ruht euch aus. (pronounced: eer root oykh owss) – You all rest.

These examples show how reflexive verbs are used in sentences with the correct reflexive pronouns.

When to Use Reflexive Verbs

In German, reflexive verbs are often used for daily routines, emotions, or actions that are done to oneself. Here are some situations where reflexive verbs are commonly used:

- **Daily Routines:** Reflexive verbs are often used to describe daily activities that we do to ourselves, like getting dressed, washing, or brushing our teeth.
  Example: **Ich wasche mich jeden Morgen.** (pronounced: ikh vah-sheh mikh yay-den mor-gen) – I wash myself every morning.

- **Emotions:** Reflexive verbs can also express emotions or feelings.
  Example: **Sie freut sich auf den Urlaub.** (pronounced: zee froy-t zikh owf den oor-laup) – She is looking forward to the vacation.

- **Health and Well-being:** Reflexive verbs are used to describe actions related to taking care of oneself.
  Example: **Er erholt sich nach dem Training.** (pronounced: air air-holt zikh nahkh dem tray-ning) – He is recovering after the training.

Reflexive Verbs in the Past Tense

To use reflexive verbs in the past tense, you need to use the helping verb **haben** (to have) with the correct reflexive pronoun and the past participle of the main verb. Here's how it works:

Subject + reflexive pronoun + haben + past participle

- **Ich habe mich geduscht.** (pronounced: ikh hah-beh mikh geh-doosht) – I took a shower.

- **Du hast dich angezogen.** (pronounced: doo hahst dikh an-ge-tzo-gen) – You got dressed.

- **Wir haben uns beeilt.** (pronounced: veer hah-ben oons beh-eye-lt) – We hurried up.

These examples show how to use reflexive verbs in the past tense with the correct helping verb and reflexive pronoun.

Non-Reflexive Use of Reflexive Verbs

Some reflexive verbs in German can also be used non-reflexively, meaning the action is done to someone or something else, not to the subject itself. Here's an example:

- Reflexive: **Ich wasche mich.** (pronounced: ikh vah-sheh mikh) – I wash myself.

- Non-Reflexive: **Ich wasche das Auto.** (pronounced: ikh vah-sheh das ow-toh) – I wash the car.

In the first sentence, "wasche" is reflexive because the subject (I) is doing the action to itself. In the second sentence, "wasche" is non-reflexive because the subject (I) is doing the action to the car.

Tips for Using Reflexive Verbs

Here are some helpful tips to remember when using reflexive verbs in German:

- Always use the correct reflexive pronoun with the verb to show that the action is being done to the subject.

- Remember that reflexive verbs are often used for daily routines, emotions, and actions related to self-care.

- Practice using reflexive verbs in both present and past tenses to get comfortable with the different forms.

- Some reflexive verbs can also be used non-reflexively, so pay attention to the context of the sentence.

Key Points to Remember

- **Reflexive Verbs:** These verbs are used when the action is done to oneself, like "sich waschen" (to wash oneself).

- **Reflexive Pronouns:** Use reflexive pronouns like "mich," "dich," "sich" to show the action is being done to the subject.

- **Daily Routines and Emotions:** Reflexive verbs are often used for daily routines, emotions, and self-care actions.

- **Past Tense:** Use "haben" with the correct reflexive pronoun and the past participle to form the past tense.

- **Non-Reflexive Use:** Some reflexive verbs can also be used non-reflexively, depending on the sentence context.

Chapter 34

Advanced Grammar: Modal Verbs

Modal verbs are special verbs in German that help us express abilities, possibilities, obligations, or desires. In English, we use modal verbs like "can," "must," "should," and "want to" to talk about what someone can do, must do, or wants to do. In German, there are six main modal verbs that work in a similar way. In this chapter, we will learn what modal verbs are, how to use them, and see examples in sentences. Let's start by understanding what modal verbs are!

What Are Modal Verbs?

Modal verbs are helper verbs that change the meaning of the main verb in a sentence. They show how the action is done – whether it is possible, necessary, allowed, or desired. The main modal verbs in German are:

- **können** (pronounced: kurn-nen) – can, to be able to

- **müssen** (pronounced: myoo-sen) – must, to have to

- **wollen** (pronounced: vol-len) – to want to

- **sollen** (pronounced: zol-len) – should, to be supposed to

- **dürfen** (pronounced: dur-fen) – may, to be allowed to

- **mögen** (pronounced: mer-gen) – to like to

These verbs help us describe what someone can, must, should, or wants to do. Let's see how they are used in sentences.

Conjugation of Modal Verbs in Present Tense

Modal verbs change depending on the subject of the sentence. Here's how the six main modal verbs are conjugated in the present tense:

- **ich kann** (pronounced: ikh kann) – I can
- **du kannst** (pronounced: doo kanst) – you can (informal)
- **er/sie/es kann** (pronounced: air/zee/es kann) – he/she/it can
- **wir können** (pronounced: veer kurn-nen) – we can
- **ihr könnt** (pronounced: eer kernnt) – you all can
- **sie/Sie können** (pronounced: zee/Zee kurn-nen) – they/you (formal) can
- **ich muss** (pronounced: ikh moos) – I must
- **du musst** (pronounced: doo moost) – you must (informal)
- **er/sie/es muss** (pronounced: air/zee/es moos) – he/she/it must
- **wir müssen** (pronounced: veer myoo-sen) – we must
- **ihr müsst** (pronounced: eer myoost) – you all must
- **sie/Sie müssen** (pronounced: zee/Zee myoo-sen) – they/you (formal) must
- **ich will** (pronounced: ikh vil) – I want
- **du willst** (pronounced: doo vilst) – you want (informal)
- **er/sie/es will** (pronounced: air/zee/es vil) – he/she/it wants
- **wir wollen** (pronounced: veer vol-len) – we want
- **ihr wollt** (pronounced: eer volt) – you all want
- **sie/Sie wollen** (pronounced: zee/Zee vol-len) – they/you (formal) want
- **ich soll** (pronounced: ikh zol) – I should
- **du sollst** (pronounced: doo zolst) – you should (informal)

- **er/sie/es soll** (pronounced: air/zee/es zol) – he/she/it should
- **wir sollen** (pronounced: veer zol-len) – we should
- **ihr sollt** (pronounced: eer zolt) – you all should
- **sie/Sie sollen** (pronounced: zee/Zee zol-len) – they/you (formal) should
- **ich darf** (pronounced: ikh darf) – I may
- **du darfst** (pronounced: doo darfst) – you may (informal)
- **er/sie/es darf** (pronounced: air/zee/es darf) – he/she/it may
- **wir dürfen** (pronounced: veer dur-fen) – we may
- **ihr dürft** (pronounced: eer durft) – you all may
- **sie/Sie dürfen** (pronounced: zee/Zee dur-fen) – they/you (formal) may
- **mögen** (to like to):
  - **ich mag** (pronounced: ikh mahg) – I like
  - **du magst** (pronounced: doo mahgst) – you like (informal)
  - **er/sie/es mag** (pronounced: air/zee/es mahg) – he/she/it likes
  - **wir mögen** (pronounced: veer mer-gen) – we like
  - **ihr mögt** (pronounced: eer merkt) – you all like
  - **sie/Sie mögen** (pronounced: zee/Zee mer-gen) – they/you (formal) like

Using Modal Verbs in Sentences

Modal verbs are always used with another verb in its infinitive form (the basic form of the v erb). The modal verb is conjugated, and the main verb stays in its infinitive form at the end of the sentence. Here are some examples:

- **Ich kann schwimmen.** (pronounced: ikh kann shvim-men) – I can swim.
- **Du musst lernen.** (pronounced: doo moost lair-nen) – You must study.
- **Er will Fußball spielen.** (pronounced: air vil foos-ball shpee-len) – He wants to play

soccer.

- **Wir dürfen ins Kino gehen.** (pronounced: veer dur-fen ins kee-noh geh-en) – We are allowed to go to the cinema.

- **Sie soll das Buch lesen.** (pronounced: zee zol das bookh lay-zen) – She should read the book.

- **Ihr mögt Eis essen.** (pronounced: eer merkt ice ess-en) – You all like to eat ice cream.

These examples show how modal verbs are used with the infinitive form of the main verb at the end of the sentence.

Modal Verbs in the Past Tense

To use modal verbs in the past tense, you use their simple past forms. Here's how the modal verbs change in the past tense:

- **können** becomes **konnte** (could)

- **müssen** becomes **musste** (had to)

- **wollen** becomes **wollte** (wanted to)

- **sollen** becomes **sollte** (should have)

- **dürfen** becomes **durfte** (was allowed to)

- **mögen** becomes **mochte** (liked to)

Here are some examples of modal verbs in the past tense:

- **Ich konnte nicht kommen.** (pronounced: ikh konn-teh nikht koh-men) – I could not come.

- **Du musstest lernen.** (pronounced: doo moos-test lair-nen) – You had to study.

- **Er wollte nach Hause gehen.** (pronounced: air vol-teh nahkh how-zeh geh-en) – He wanted to go home.

- **Wir durften bleiben.** (pronounced: veer durf-ten bly-ben) – We were allowed to stay.

- **Sie sollte das Buch lesen.** (pronounced: zee zol-teh das bookh lay-zen) – She should have read the book.

Using Modal Verbs with Negatives

You can also use modal verbs with negatives to express things that are not allowed, not possible, or not desired. Here's how it works:

- **Ich darf nicht gehen.** (pronounced: ikh darf nikht geh-en) – I am not allowed to go.

- **Du kannst nicht schwimmen.** (pronounced: doo kanst nikht shvim-men) – You cannot swim.

- **Wir wollen nicht spielen.** (pronounced: veer vol-len nikht shpee-len) – We do not want to play.

These sentences show how to use modal verbs with negative forms to express prohibition, inability, or unwillingness.

Key Points to Remember

- **Modal Verbs:** These verbs help express abilities, possibilities, obligations, or desires like "können" (can) or "müssen" (must).

- **Conjugation:** Modal verbs change according to the subject, and the main verb stays in its infinitive form at the end of the sentence.

- **Past Tense Forms:** Modal verbs have their own past tense forms, like "konnte" (could) or "musste" (had to).

- **Using Negatives:** Use "nicht" with modal verbs to express something that is not allowed, not possible, or not wanted.

- **Practice:** Use modal verbs to describe what you can, must, should, want, or like to do!

Chapter 35

Advanced Vocabulary: Abstract Nouns

Abstract nouns are words that name things you cannot see, touch, or hold. They refer to ideas, feelings, qualities, or concepts that exist in our minds. For example, words like "happiness," "freedom," and "love" are abstract nouns. These words describe things that you can feel or think about but not touch or see. In this chapter, we will learn some important abstract nouns in German and how to use them in sentences. Let's start by understanding what abstract nouns are!

What Are Abstract Nouns?

Abstract nouns are different from concrete nouns. Concrete nouns are things you can see, touch, or hold, like "apple" or "car." Abstract nouns, on the other hand, represent ideas or feelings, like "friendship" or "courage." In German, just like in English, we use abstract nouns to talk about thoughts, emotions, qualities, and more.

Here are some common abstract nouns in German:

- **die Freiheit** (pronounced: dee fry-hite) – freedom
- **die Liebe** (pronounced: dee lee-beh) – love
- **die Freundschaft** (pronounced: dee froind-shaft) – friendship
- **der Mut** (pronounced: dair moot) – courage
- **die Hoffnung** (pronounced: dee hoff-noong) – hope
- **die Geduld** (pronounced: dee geh-doolt) – patience
- **das Glück** (pronounced: das glueck) – happiness, luck

- **die Traurigkeit** (pronounced: dee trow-rig-kite) – sadness
- **die Gerechtigkeit** (pronounced: dee geh-rek-tik-kite) – justice
- **die Wahrheit** (pronounced: dee var-hite) – truth

These are some of the common abstract nouns that you might use when speaking or writing in German. Let's learn how to use them in sentences.

Using Abstract Nouns in Sentences

Just like other nouns, abstract nouns in German can be used in sentences as the subject or the object. Here are some examples of sentences using abstract nouns:

- **Freiheit ist wichtig.** (pronounced: fry-hite ist vik-tig) – Freedom is important.
- **Liebe macht glücklich.** (pronounced: lee-beh makht gluek-likh) – Love makes one happy.
- **Freundschaft ist ein Geschenk.** (pronounced: froind-shaft ist ine ge-shenk) – Friendship is a gift.
- **Mut hilft uns, unsere Ziele zu erreichen.** (pronounced: moot hilt oons, oon-zeh-reh tsee-leh tsoo air-righ-en) – Courage helps us reach our goals.
- **Hoffnung gibt uns Kraft.** (pronounced: hoff-noong geebt oons kraft) – Hope gives us strength.

These sentences show how abstract nouns can be used to talk about concepts or feelings.

Abstract Nouns and Their Articles

Just like other German nouns, abstract nouns have genders and are used with definite articles. Here's a quick reminder of the definite articles in German:

- **der** (pronounced: dair) – for masculine nouns
- **die** (pronounced: dee) – for feminine nouns
- **das** (pronounced: das) – for neuter nouns

Most abstract nouns in German are feminine and use the article **die**, like "die Freiheit" (freedom) and "die Liebe" (love). However, some are masculine or neuter, like "der Mut" (courage) and "das Glück" (happiness, luck).

Common Abstract Nouns in Everyday Language

Let's look at more examples of how to use abstract nouns in everyday conversations:

- **Die Geduld ist eine Tugend.** (pronounced: dee geh-doolt ist eye-neh too-gent) – Patience is a virtue.

- **Wahrheit ist immer wichtig.** (pronounced: var-hite ist im-mer vik-tig) – Truth is always important.

- **Glück bedeutet, die kleinen Dinge zu genießen.** (pronounced: gluek beh-doy-tet, dee klai-nen ding-eh tsoo ge-nee-sen) – Happiness means enjoying the little things.

- **Gerechtigkeit soll für alle gelten.** (pronounced: geh-rek-tik-kite zol fuer ah-leh gelt-en) – Justice should be for everyone.

- **Traurigkeit gehört zum Leben.** (pronounced: trow-rig-kite geh-hoert tsoom lay-ben) – Sadness is a part of life.

These sentences show how abstract nouns can be used to express deeper thoughts and ideas.

Abstract Nouns for Emotions

Many abstract nouns are used to describe emotions or feelings. Here are some important German nouns related to emotions:

- **die Angst** (pronounced: dee angst) – fear

- **die Freude** (pronounced: dee froi-deh) – joy

- **der Ärger** (pronounced: dair air-ger) – anger

- **die Zufriedenheit** (pronounced: dee tsoo-free-den-hite) – contentment

- **die Verzweiflung** (pronounced: dee fer-tsvife-loong) – despair

These nouns help describe different emotional states. Here are some examples:

- **Angst ist normal.** (pronounced: angst ist nor-mal) – Fear is normal.

- **Freude macht das Leben schön.** (pronounced: froi-deh makht das lay-ben shern) – Joy makes life beautiful.

- **Ärger kann schnell verschwinden.** (pronounced: air-ger kann shnell fer-shvin-den) – Anger can disappear quickly.

- **Zufriedenheit kommt von innen.** (pronounced: tsoo-free-den-hite kommt fon in-nen) – Contentment comes from within.

- **Verzweiflung sollte niemals die Hoffnung zerstören.** (pronounced: fer-tsvife-loong zol-teh nee-mahls dee hoff-noong tser-shto-ren) – Despair should never destroy hope.

These examples help you use abstract nouns to talk about feelings and emotions.

Abstract Nouns for Qualities and Concepts

Abstract nouns are also used to describe qualities or concepts that are important in life. Here are some examples:

- **die Ehrlichkeit** (pronounced: dee air-likh-kite) – honesty

- **die Toleranz** (pronounced: dee toh-leh-rants) – tolerance

- **die Verantwortung** (pronounced: dee fer-ant-vor-toong) – responsibility

- **die Weisheit** (pronounced: dee vise-hite) – wisdom

- **die Kreativität** (pronounced : dee kreh-ah-tee-vi-taet) – creativity

Here are some sentences using these nouns:

- **Ehrlichkeit ist die beste Politik.** (pronounced: air-likh-kite ist dee bes-teh poh-lee-teek) – Honesty is the best policy.

- **Toleranz hilft, Frieden zu schaffen.** (pronounced: toh-leh-rants hilt, free-den tsoo shahf-fen) – Tolerance helps create peace.

- **Verantwortung ist wichtig für ein gutes Leben.** (pronounced: fer-ant-vor-toong ist vik-tig fuer ine goo-tes lay-ben) – Responsibility is important for a good life.

- **Weisheit kommt mit Erfahrung.** (pronounced: vise-hite kommt mit air-fahr-oong) – Wisdom comes with experience.

- **Kreativität bringt neue Ideen.** (pronounced: kreh-ah-tee-vi-taet bringt noi-eh ee-day-en) – Creativity brings new ideas.

These examples show how abstract nouns can be used to describe qualities and concepts that are important in life.

Key Points to Remember

- **Abstract Nouns:** These nouns describe ideas, feelings, qualities, or concepts, like "Freiheit" (freedom) or "Liebe" (love).

- **Use in Sentences:** Abstract nouns can be used as subjects or objects in sentences, just like other nouns.

- **Articles Matter:** Remember to use the correct articles: "der," "die," or "das" based on the noun's gender.

- **Emotion Words:** Many abstract nouns describe emotions or feelings, like "Freude" (joy) or "Ärger" (anger).

- **Qualities and Concepts:** Abstract nouns are also used to describe qualities like "Ehrlichkeit" (honesty) or "Kreativität" (creativity).

Chapter 36

Formal and Informal Language

When learning German, it's important to know that there are two main ways to speak: formally and informally. Formal language is used when you are speaking to someone you don't know well, like a teacher, a stranger, or someone older. Informal language is used with friends, family, and people you know well. Understanding when to use formal and informal language will help you communicate politely and correctly in different situations. In this chapter, we will learn how to use both formal and informal language in German, the rules for each, and examples to help you practice.

Formal vs. Informal: When to Use Them?

In English, we usually use the same words whether we are speaking formally or informally. For example, you might say "you" to both your friend and your teacher. However, in German, the way you speak changes depending on who you are talking to.

Here are some situations where you would use formal or informal language in German:

- **Formal Language:** Use formal language when speaking to adults you don't know well, in professional settings, with teachers, or with people in positions of authority.
  Example: Talking to your teacher, a store clerk, or a police officer.

- **Informal Language:** Use informal language with friends, family members, classmates, or anyone you know well.
  Example: Talking to your best friend, your sibling, or your cousin.

Let's look at some of the key differences between formal and informal language in German.

Pronouns: "Du" vs. "Sie"

One of the main differences between formal and informal German is the use of pronouns. The pronouns "du" (you, informal) and "Sie" (you, formal) are used depending on the level of formality. Here's how to use them:

- **Du** (pronounced: doo) – This is the informal way to say "you." It is used with friends, family, and people you know well.

- **Sie** (pronounced: zee) – This is the formal way to say "you." It is always capitalized and is used when speaking to someone in a polite or formal manner.

Here are some examples:

- **Du bist mein Freund.** (pronounced: doo bist mine froint) – You are my friend. (informal)

- **Wie heißen Sie?** (pronounced: vee hy-sen zee) – What is your name? (formal)

Notice how "du" is used informally with a friend, while "Sie" is used formally when asking for someone's name politely.

Formal and Informal Greetings

German also has different greetings for formal and informal situations. Here are some common greetings and when to use them:

- **Hallo** (pronounced: hah-loh) – Hello (informal)
  Use "Hallo" when greeting friends, family, or people you know well.

- **Guten Tag** (pronounced: goo-ten tahk) – Good day (formal)
  Use "Guten Tag" when greeting someone formally, like a teacher or a stranger.

- **Tschüss** (pronounced: chews) – Bye (informal)
  Use "Tschüss" when saying goodbye to friends or family.

- **Auf Wiedersehen** (pronounced: owf vee-der-zay-en) – Goodbye (formal)
  Use "Auf Wiedersehen" when saying goodbye in a formal situation.

These greetings help you know how to start and end conversations politely in different settings.

Formal and Informal Questions

When asking questions in German, the formality of the question changes depending on whether you use "du" or "Sie." Here are some examples:

- **Informal:**
  Wie geht's dir? (pronounced: vee gets deer) – How are you? (informal)

- **Formal:**
  Wie geht es Ihnen? (pronounced: vee gate es ee-nen) – How are you? (formal)

Notice how the informal question uses "dir" (you, informal), while the formal question uses "Ihnen" (you, formal). Knowing these differences will help you sound polite in various situations.

Formal and Informal Commands

Commands in German also change based on formality. Here's how to give commands formally and informally:

- **Informal Command:**
  Komm her! (pronounced: komm hair) – Come here! (informal)

- **Formal Command:**
  Kommen Sie her! (pronounced: komm-en zee hair) – Come here! (formal)

When giving a command informally, you just use the verb's root, like "komm." For formal commands, you use the verb in its full form with "Sie," like "kommen Sie."

Other Differences in Formal and Informal Language

Besides pronouns, greetings, questions, and commands, there are a few other differences between formal and informal German:

- **Titles and Last Names:** In formal situations, Germans often use titles (like Herr or Frau) and last names. For example, you might say "Herr Müller" (Mr. Müller) or "Frau Schmidt" (Mrs. Schmidt). In informal settings, you usually use first names.

- **Polite Expressions:** In formal German, people often use polite expressions like "bitte" (please) and "danke" (thank you) more frequently to show respect.

- **Sentence Structure:** Formal sentences might use more complex structures and complete sentences, while informal speech may be simpler and more relaxed.

Practice Using Formal and Informal Language

To get used to using both formal and informal language in German, here are a few practice ideas:

- Practice greeting your friends and family using "Hallo" and saying goodbye with

"Tschüss."

- Try asking formal questions like "Wie heißen Sie?" when pretending to speak to a teacher or stranger.

- Use polite expressions like "bitte" and "danke" in both formal and informal situations to show respect.

These exercises will help you become more comfortable with using formal and informal German appropriately.

Why Is It Important to Know Formal and Informal Language?

Knowing the difference between formal and informal language in German is important because it shows respect and politeness. Using the right form helps you fit into different social situations and communicate clearly with others. For example, if you speak formally to a teacher, they will see that you are respectful. If you speak informally to your friends, they will know you are comfortable with them.

Key Points to Remember

- **Pronouns Matter:** Use "du" for informal situations and "Sie" for formal situations.

- **Greetings Change:** "Hallo" is informal; "Guten Tag" is formal.

- **Questions and Commands:** Adjust your questions and commands based on whether you are being formal or informal.

- **Politeness Counts:** Use titles, polite expressions, and proper sentence structures in formal situations.

- **Practice Both:** Practice using both forms to know when to speak formally and informally.

Chapter 37

Cultural Etiquette and Customs

When you are learning a new language like German, it's not just about the words and grammar; it's also important to learn about the culture and customs of the people who speak that language. Knowing how to behave, greet people, and show respect in a different culture helps you communicate better and make friends more easily. In this chapter, we will learn some important aspects of German cultural etiquette and customs, and understand how to behave in different situations. Let's explore how to be polite and respectful in Germany!

Greetings and Introductions

In Germany, greetings are an important part of everyday life. When you meet someone, it is customary to greet them with a handshake and direct eye contact. Germans appreciate it when people are polite and respectful.

- **Handshake:** A firm handshake is a common way to greet someone in Germany. Make sure to make eye contact while shaking hands. This shows respect and confidence.

- **Formal Greetings:** When meeting someone for the first time or in a formal setting, use "Guten Tag" (pronounced: goo-ten tahk) – Good day. You can also say "Guten Morgen" (pronounced: goo-ten mor-gen) – Good morning, or "Guten Abend" (pronounced: goo-ten ah-bent) – Good evening.

- **Informal Greetings:** With friends or family, you can use "Hallo" (pronounced: hah-loh) – Hello, or "Hi" (pronounced just like in English).

- **Introductions:** When introducing yourself, say "Ich heiße [your name]" (pronounced: ikh hy-seh) – My name is [your name]. To ask someone their name, you can say, "Wie heißen Sie?" (pronounced: vee hy-sen zee) – What is your name? (formal), or "Wie heißt du?" (pronounced: vee hy-st doo) – What is your name? (informal).

By using proper greetings and introductions, you show respect and friendliness when meeting people in Germany.

Politeness and Respect

Politeness is very important in German culture. Here are some key points to keep in mind:

- **Use "Bitte" and "Danke":** Always use the word "Bitte" (pronounced: bit-teh) – Please, when asking for something, and "Danke" (pronounced: dank-eh) – Thank you, when you receive something or someone helps you.

- **Respect Personal Space:** Germans value personal space. It is polite to maintain a comfortable distance when talking to someone and avoid touching them too much, especially if you do not know them well.

- **Address People Formally:** When speaking to someone you do not know well, use "Sie" (pronounced: zee) – the formal "you." Only use "du" (pronounced: doo) – the informal "you," if the person invites you to do so.

By following these simple rules, you show that you understand and respect German customs and culture.

Table Manners

When eating in Germany, there are specific manners to follow to show politeness and respect. Here are some tips:

- **Wait Before Eating:** It is polite to wait until everyone is served before you start eating. You should also wait for the host or hostess to say "Guten Appetit" (pronounced: goo-ten ah-peh-teet) – Enjoy your meal, before you begin.

- **Use Utensils Properly:** Germans typically use a knife in the right hand and a fork in the left hand while eating. Do not switch hands, and do not cut all your food at once. Cut one piece at a time.

- **Keep Your Hands Visible:** When eating, it is polite to keep your hands visible on the table but avoid putting your elbows on the table. Place your hands on the sides of the plate.

- **Finish Your Plate:** It is considered polite to finish all the food on your plate, as leaving food can be seen as wasteful.

- **Say "Prost!":** When drinking with others, say "Prost!" (pronounced: prohst) – Cheers, before taking a sip. Make sure to make eye contact with each person at the table while saying it.

These table manners help you show respect and politeness when sharing a meal in Germany.

Customs and Traditions

Germany has many customs and traditions that are celebrated throughout the year. Here are a few important ones to know:

- **Oktoberfest:** (pronounced: ok-toh-ber-fest) – This is a famous festival celebrated in Munich every year from late September to the first weekend in October. People wear traditional clothes like **Lederhosen** (pronounced: lay-der-hoh-zen) for men and **Dirndl** (pronounced: dihrn-del) for women, and enjoy beer, food, and music.

- **Christmas Markets:** (pronounced: kris-mahs markts) – In December, many cities in Germany have Christmas markets where people buy gifts, enjoy traditional foods like **Bratwurst** (pronounced: braht-voorst) and **Lebkuchen** (pronounced: layb-koo-khen), and drink hot spiced wine called **Glühwein** (pronounced: glew-vine).

- **Karnival:** (pronounced: kar-ni-val) – Also known as Fasching or Fastnacht, this is a festival that happens before Lent in February or March. People wear costumes, have parades, and celebrate with music and dancing.

- **New Year's Eve – Silvester:** (pronounced: zil-ves-ter) – Germans celebrate New Year's Eve with fireworks, parties, and special foods like **Raclette** (pronounced: ra-klet) and **Fondue** (pronounced: fon-doo).

Understanding these customs and traditions will help you appreciate German culture and participate in celebrations when you visit Germany.

Gifts and Hospitality

When you visit someone's home in Germany, it is polite to bring a small gift for the host, such as flowers, chocolates, or wine. Here are some things to remember about giving gifts:

- **Bring a Small Gift:** Bringing a small gift shows that you are thankful for the invitation. For example, you might bring a bouquet of flowers or a box of chocolates.

- **Give Flowers Correctly:** When giving flowers, make sure to give an odd number, like

3, 5, or 7. Even numbers of flowers are usually given at funerals.

- **Say "Danke" and "Bitte":** Always thank your host when you arrive and when you leave. Saying "Danke" (thank you) and "Bitte" (please) shows respect and gratitude.

These tips will help you be a polite guest and show appreciation when visiting someone's home in Germany.

Punctuality

In Germany, being on time is very important. Germans are known for their punctuality and being late is considered impolite. Here are some tips to help you be on time:

- **Arrive Early:** Try to arrive 5 to 10 minutes early for appointments or meetings. This shows that you are respectful of other people's time.

- **Call if You Are Late:** If you are going to be late, make sure to call ahead and apologize. This shows that you care about other people's time and are considerate.

By being punctual, you show respect for the people you are meeting and the time they have given you.

Using Titles and Last Names

In Germany, people often use titles like "Herr" (Mr.) or "Frau" (Mrs.) along with last names in formal situations. This is a sign of respect. Here are some examples:

- **Herr Müller:** (pronounced: hair muel-er) – Mr. Müller

- **Frau Schmidt:** (pronounced: frow shmidt) – Mrs. Schmidt

Using titles like "Herr" and "Frau" shows that you respect the person you are speaking to, especially if you don't know them well.

Key Points to Remember

- **Greetings Matter:** Use formal greetings like "Guten Tag" and a firm handshake when meeting people.

- **Politeness is Key:** Use "Bitte" and "Danke," and respect personal space to show politeness.

- **Table Manners:** Wait before eating, use utensils properly, and say "Prost!" when drinking with others.

- **Be Punctual:** Arrive on time for appointments, and if late, call ahead to apologize.

- **Use Titles:** Address people with "Herr" or "Frau" and their last name in formal situations.

Chapter 38

Science and Technology Vocabulary

Learning science and technology words in German can be fun and exciting! These words will help you talk about things like computers, space, experiments, and more. In this chapter, we will learn some common science and technology vocabulary that you might use in school or everyday life. Let's start by looking at some basic words and phrases that are important to know.

Basic Science Vocabulary

Here are some basic science words in German that you might hear in your science class:

- **die Wissenschaft** (pronounced: dee vis-en-shaft) – science
- **das Experiment** (pronounced: das eks-pair-i-ment) – experiment
- **die Chemie** (pronounced: dee she-mee) – chemistry
- **die Biologie** (pronounced: dee bee-oh-loh-gee) – biology
- **die Physik** (pronounced: dee fyoo-zeek) – physics
- **das Labor** (pronounced: das lah-bor) – laboratory
- **der Wissenschaftler** (pronounced: dair vis-en-shaft-ler) – scientist (male)
- **die Wissenschaftlerin** (pronounced: dee vis-en-shaft-le-rin) – scientist (female)

These words will help you talk about different subjects in science and the people who work in them. Let's see how we can use them in sentences:

- **Wir machen ein Experiment im Labor.** (pronounced: veer mah-khen ine eks-pair-i-ment im lah-bor) – We are doing an experiment in the laboratory.

- **Die Biologie ist die Wissenschaft des Lebens.** (pronounced: dee bee-oh-loh-gee ist dee vis-en-shaft des lay-bens) – Biology is the science of life.

- **Der Wissenschaftler studiert die Chemie.** (pronounced: dair vis-en-shaft-ler shtoo-deert dee she-mee) – The scientist studies chemistry.

Using these basic words will help you understand and discuss scientific topics in German.

Technology Vocabulary

Technology is a big part of our lives today. Here are some German words related to technology:

- **der Computer** (pronounced: dair kom-pyoo-ter) – computer
- **das Internet** (pronounced: das in-ter-net) – internet
- **die Technologie** (pronounced: dee tek-no-loh-gee) – technology
- **das Handy** (pronounced: das han-dee) – cell phone
- **der Roboter** (pronounced: dair roh-boh-ter) – robot
- **die Software** (pronounced: dee soft-vair) – software
- **die Hardware** (pronounced: dee hard-vair) – hardware
- **der Bildschirm** (pronounced: dair bild-shirm) – screen/monitor

These words will help you talk about computers, phones, and other technology. Here are some example sentences:

- **Ich benutze den Computer, um meine Hausaufgaben zu machen.** (pronounced: ikh beh-noot-zeh den kom-pyoo-ter, oom my-neh hows-owf-gah-ben tsoo mah-khen) – I use the computer to do my homework.

- **Das Handy ist sehr praktisch.** (pronounced: das han-dee ist zair prak-tish) – The cell phone is very practical.

- **Der Roboter hilft uns im Alltag.** (pronounced: dair roh-boh-ter hilt oons im ahlt-tahg) – The robot helps us in everyday life.

These sentences show how to use technology-related vocabulary in conversation.

Space and Astronomy Vocabulary

If you are interested in space and the stars, here are some useful words in German:

- **das Universum** (pronounced: das oo-nee-ver-soom) – universe
- **der Planet** (pronounced: dair plah-net) – planet
- **die Sonne** (pronounced: dee zon-neh) – sun
- **der Mond** (pronounced: dair mohnd) – moon
- **der Stern** (pronounced: dair shtairn) – star
- **die Astronomie** (pronounced: dee ah-stro-no-mee) – astronomy
- **der Astronaut** (pronounced: dair ah-stroh-nowt) – astronaut (male)
- **die Astronautin** (pronounced: dee ah-stroh-now-tin) – astronaut (female)

Here are some sentences using space vocabulary:

- **Der Astronaut fliegt zum Mond.** (pronounced: dair ah-stroh-nowt fleegt tsoom mohnd) – The astronaut flies to the moon.
- **Wir lernen über die Sterne im Universum.** (pronounced: veer lair-nen oo-ber dee shtair-neh im oo-nee-ver-soom) – We learn about the stars in the universe.
- **Die Sonne ist ein Stern.** (pronounced: dee zon-neh ist ine shtairn) – The sun is a star.

These words and sentences will help you talk about space and astronomy in German.

Environmental Science Vocabulary

Understanding the environment is also an important part of science. Here are some German words related to environmental science:

- **die Umwelt** (pronounced: dee oom-velt) – environment
- **das Klima** (pronounced: das klee-mah) – climate
- **der Umweltschutz** (pronounced: dair oom-velt-shoots) – environmental protection

- **die Verschmutzung** (pronounced: dee fair-shmoot-zoong) – pollution

- **das Recycling** (pronounced: das ree-sigh-klin-g) – recycling

- **die Energie** (pronounced: dee eh-ner-gee) – energy

- **das Wasser** (pronounced: das vah-ser) – water

- **die Luft** (pronounced: dee looft) – air

These words can be used to talk about important environmental topics:

- **Wir müssen die Umwelt schützen.** (pronounced: veer myoo-sen dee oom-velt shuet-sen) – We must protect the environment.

- **Recycling hilft, die Verschmutzung zu reduzieren.** (pronounced: ree-sigh-klin-g hilt, dee fair-shmoot-zoong tsoo reh-doo-tsee-ren) – Recycling helps to reduce pollution.

- **Das Klima verändert sich.** (pronounced: das klee-mah feyr-end-ert zikh) – The climate is changing.

These sentences will help you discuss environmental science topics in German.

Useful Phrases for Science and Technology

Here are some useful phrases to help you talk about science and technology in German:

- **Wie funktioniert das?** (pronounced: vee foonk-tsyoh-neert das) – How does that work?

- **Ich habe eine Frage zur Wissenschaft.** (pronounced: ikh hah-beh eye-neh frah-geh tsoor vis-en-shaft) – I have a question about science.

- **Was ist deine Lieblingswissenschaft?** (pronounced: vas ist dye-neh lee-blingz-vis-en-shaft) – What is your favorite science?

These phrases will help you communicate effectively in a science or technology setting.

Key Points to Remember

- **Basic Science Words:** Learn words like "Wissenschaft" (science) and "Experiment" (experiment) to talk about science topics.

- **Technology Terms:** Use words like "Computer" (computer) and "Handy" (cell phone) to discuss technology.

- **Space Vocabulary:** Know words like "Planet" (planet) and "Astronaut" (astronaut) to talk about space.

- **Environmental Words:** Use terms like "Umwelt" (environment) and "Recycling" (recycling) for environmental science.

- **Useful Phrases:** Practice phrases like "Wie funktioniert das?" (How does that work?) to engage in science conversations.

Chapter 39

Business and Economics Vocabulary

Understanding business and economics vocabulary in German can help you learn how people talk about money, trade, jobs, and the economy. These words are important in everyday life because they help us understand how businesses work and how people earn and spend money. In this chapter, we will learn some common business and economics words in German and see how to use them in sentences. Let's start by learning some basic vocabulary!

Basic Business Vocabulary

Here are some basic words in German related to business:

- **das Geschäft** (pronounced: das ge-shaft) – business, shop
- **die Firma** (pronounced: dee feer-mah) – company, firm
- **der Chef** (pronounced: dair shef) – boss (male)
- **die Chefin** (pronounced: dee she-fin) – boss (female)
- **der Kunde** (pronounced: dair koon-deh) – customer (male)
- **die Kundin** (pronounced: dee koon-din) – customer (female)
- **das Produkt** (pronounced: das proh-dukt) – product
- **die Dienstleistung** (pronounced: dee deensht-lye-stoong) – service

These words are often used in conversations about businesses and how they operate. Here are some example sentences:

- **Die Firma verkauft viele Produkte.** (pronounced: dee feer-mah fer-kowft fee-leh proh-duk-teh) – The company sells many products.

- **Der Kunde ist immer König.** (pronounced: dair koon-deh ist im-mer ker-nig) – The customer is always king.

- **Unsere Chefin ist sehr freundlich.** (pronounced: oon-zeh-reh she-fin ist zair froint-likh) – Our boss is very friendly.

These sentences show how to use basic business words in everyday conversations.

Economics Vocabulary

Economics is the study of how people use resources, make goods, and trade with others. Here are some important German words related to economics:

- **die Wirtschaft** (pronounced: dee veer-shaft) – economy

- **das Geld** (pronounced: das gelt) – money

- **der Preis** (pronounced: dair price) – price

- **die Nachfrage** (pronounced: dee nahk-frah-geh) – demand

- **das Angebot** (pronounced: das ahn-geh-boat) – supply, offer

- **der Markt** (pronounced: dair markt) – market

- **die Inflation** (pronounced: dee in-flah-tsion) – inflation

- **das Einkommen** (pronounced: das ine-kom-men) – income

These words help us understand how the economy works. Here are some examples:

- **Die Nachfrage nach Bio-Produkten steigt.** (pronounced: dee nahk-frah-geh nahkh bee-oh-proh-duk-ten shtygt) – The demand for organic products is rising.

- **Der Preis für Milch ist gesunken.** (pronounced: dair price fuer milkh ist geh-zoon-ken) – The price for milk has decreased.

- **Die Inflation ist ein großes Problem.** (pronounced: dee in-flah-tsion ist ine groh-ses pro-blehm) – Inflation is a big problem.

These sentences help you use economics words to talk about everyday topics.

Jobs and Employment Vocabulary

Jobs and employment are important parts of business and economics. Here are some German words related to jobs:

- **der Job** (pronounced: dair yob) – job
- **die Arbeit** (pronounced: dee ar-bite) – work
- **der Arbeitnehmer** (pronounced: dair arbite-neh-mer) – employee (male)
- **die Arbeitnehmerin** (pronounced: dee arbite-neh-me-rin) – employee (female)
- **der Arbeitgeber** (pronounced: dair arbite-gay-ber) – employer
- **das Gehalt** (pronounced: das geh-hahlt) – salary
- **die Karriere** (pronounced: dee ka-ree-air-reh) – career

These words are useful when talking about jobs or work. Here are some example sentences:

- **Ich suche einen neuen Job.** (pronounced: ikh zoo-khe ine-noy-en yob) – I am looking for a new job.
- **Sie hat eine gute Karriere gemacht.** (pronounced: zee haht eye-neh goo-teh ka-ree-air-reh geh-mahkt) – She has made a good career.
- **Der Arbeitnehmer bekommt ein gutes Gehalt.** (pronounced: dair arbite-neh-mer beh-kommt ine goo-tes geh-hahlt) – The employee receives a good salary.

These sentences help you talk about work and employment in German.

Money and Banking Vocabulary

Money and banking are also important parts of business. Here are some German words related to money and banking:

- **die Bank** (pronounced: dee bahnk) – bank
- **das Konto** (pronounced: das kon-toh) – account
- **der Kredit** (pronounced: dair kreh-deet) – credit
- **das Bargeld** (pronounced: das bar-gelt) – cash

BUSINESS AND ECONOMICS VOCABULARY

- **die Überweisung** (pronounced: dee oo-ber-vi-soong) – transfer

- **die Investition** (pronounced: dee in-vest-ee-tsion) – investment

- **die Aktie** (pronounced: dee ak-tsee-eh) – stock

Here are some sentences using these words:

- **Ich habe ein Konto bei der Bank eröffnet.** (pronounced: ikh hah-beh ine kon-toh by dair bahnk air-oeff-net) – I opened an account at the bank.

- **Er hat in Aktien investiert.** (pronounced: air haht in ak-tsee-en in-vest-eert) – He has invested in stocks.

- **Wir zahlen mit Bargeld.** (pronounced: veer tsah-len mit bar-gelt) – We pay with cash.

These examples will help you discuss money and banking in German.

International Trade Vocabulary

International trade is when countries buy and sell goods and services to each other. Here are some German words related to international trade:

- **der Handel** (pronounced: dair han-del) – trade

- **der Export** (pronounced: dair eks-port) – export

- **der Import** (pronounced: dair im-port) – import

- **die Zollgebühren** (pronounced: dee tsoll-ge-boo-ren) – customs duties

- **der Vertrag** (pronounced: dair fer-trahg) – contract

- **die Währung** (pronounced: dee vehr-oong) – currency

Here are some example sentences:

- **Deutschland exportiert viele Autos.** (pronounced: doitsh-land eks-por-teert fee-leh ow-tos) – Germany exports many cars.

- **Der Import von Obst ist gestiegen.** (pronounced: dair im-port fon obst ist geh-shtie-gen) – The import of fruits has increased.

- **Wir müssen die Zollgebühren bezahlen.** (pronounced: veer myoo-sen dee tsoll-ge-boo-ren beh-tsah-len) – We have to pay the customs duties.

These sentences help you understand and discuss international trade in German.

Useful Phrases for Business and Economics

Here are some useful phrases that can help you talk about business and economics in German:

- **Wie viel kostet das?** (pronounced: vee feel kohst-et das) – How much does that cost?

- **Ich möchte eine Investition machen.** (pronounced: ikh merkh-teh eye-neh in-vest-ee-tsion mah-khen) – I want to make an investment.

- **Was ist der Preis für dieses Produkt?** (pronounced: vas ist dair price fuer dee-zes proh-dukt) – What is the price of this product?

These phrases will help you engage in conversations about business and economics topics in German.

Key Points to Remember

- **Basic Business Words:** Learn words like "Firma" (company) and "Produkt" (product) to talk about business topics.

- **Economics Terms:** Use words like "Wirtschaft" (economy) and "Preis" (price) to discuss economic concepts.

- **Job Vocabulary:** Know words like "Job" (job) and "Arbeit" (work) to talk about employment.

- **Money and Banking:** Use terms like "Bank" (bank) and "Konto" (account) for financial discussions.

- **Trade Words:** Understand terms like "Export" (export) and "Import" (import) to talk about international trade.

Chapter 40

Media and Communications Vocabulary

Learning about media and communications in German is important because it helps you understand how people share information, news, and entertainment. This vocabulary will help you talk about newspapers, television, social media, and other ways people communicate. In this chapter, we will explore some common media and communications words in German and learn how to use them in sentences. Let's start with some basic words related to media!

Basic Media Vocabulary

Here are some basic German words related to media:

- **die Medien** (pronounced: dee may-dee-en) – media

- **die Zeitung** (pronounced: dee tsai-toong) – newspaper

- **das Fernsehen** (pronounced: das fairn-zay-en) – television

- **der Rundfunk** (pronounced: dair roond-foonk) – radio broadcasting

- **der Journalist** (pronounced: dair yohr-nah-list) – journalist (male)

- **die Journalistin** (pronounced: dee yohr-nah-lis-tin) – journalist (female)

- **die Nachrichten** (pronounced: dee nah-rikh-ten) – news

- **der Artikel** (pronounced: dair ar-tee-kel) – article

These words are commonly used in conversations about news and media. Here are some examples:

- **Ich lese jeden Morgen die Zeitung.** (pronounced: ikh lay-zeh yay-den mor-gen dee tsai-toong) – I read the newspaper every morning.

- **Die Nachrichten kommen um acht Uhr.** (pronounced: dee nah-rikh-ten koh-men oom ahkt oor) – The news comes on at eight o'clock.

- **Der Journalist schreibt einen Artikel.** (pronounced: dair yohr-nah-list shribt eye-nen ar-tee-kel) – The journalist is writing an article.

These sentences will help you use basic media vocabulary in everyday situations.

Digital Media Vocabulary

Digital media is very popular today, and here are some German words related to it:

- **das Internet** (pronounced: das in-ter-net) – internet

- **die Webseite** (pronounced: dee veb-sy-teh) – website

- **die E-Mail** (pronounced: dee ee-mail) – email

- **das soziale Netzwerk** (pronounced: das zoht-see-ah-leh netz-vairk) – social network

- **der Blog** (pronounced: dair blog) – blog

- **das Video** (pronounced: das vee-dee-oh) – video

- **der Podcast** (pronounced: dair pod-kast) – podcast

These words help you talk about online activities and digital content. Here are some example sentences:

- **Ich schreibe eine E-Mail an meinen Freund.** (pronounced: ikh shribe eye-neh ee-mail an my-nen froind) – I am writing an email to my friend.

- **Wir hören einen Podcast über Geschichte.** (pronounced: veer hoer-en eye-nen pod-kast oo-ber geh-shikh-teh) – We are listening to a podcast about history.

- **Sie hat einen Blog über Reisen.** (pronounced: zee haht eye-nen blog oo-ber rye-zen) – She has a blog about travel.

These sentences show how digital media vocabulary is used in everyday conversations.

Communication Tools Vocabulary

Communication tools help people share messages and connect with each other. Here are some German words for common communication tools:

- **das Telefon** (pronounced: das tel-eh-fohn) – telephone
- **das Handy** (pronounced: das han-dee) – cell phone
- **der Computer** (pronounced: dair kom-pyoo-ter) – computer
- **die Kamera** (pronounced: dee kah-meh-rah) – camera
- **das Mikrofon** (pronounced: das mee-kroh-fohn) – microphone
- **die Tastatur** (pronounced: dee tahs-tah-toor) – keyboard
- **der Drucker** (pronounced: dair droo-ker) – printer

Here are some sentences using these words:

- **Ich benutze das Handy, um mit meinen Eltern zu sprechen.** (pronounced: ikh beh-noot-zeh das han-dee, oom mit my-nen el-tern tsoo shpre-khen) – I use the cell phone to talk to my parents.
- **Der Journalist braucht eine Kamera für die Fotos.** (pronounced: dair yohr-nah-list browkht eye-neh kah-meh-rah fuer dee foh-tohs) – The journalist needs a camera for the photos.
- **Wir drucken die Dokumente mit dem Drucker.** (pronounced: veer droo-ken dee doh-koo-men-teh mit dem droo-ker) – We print the documents with the printer.

These examples show how to use words for communication tools in sentences.

Broadcasting and Journalism Vocabulary

Broadcasting and journalism are important parts of the media. Here are some German words related to broadcasting and journalism:

- **die Sendung** (pronounced: dee zen-doong) – broadcast, show
- **der Kanal** (pronounced: dair kah-nahl) – channel
- **die Reportage** (pronounced: dee reh-por-tah-jeh) – report

- **die Presse** (pronounced: dee pres-seh) – press

- **das Interview** (pronounced: das in-ter-vyoo) – interview

- **der Korrespondent** (pronounced: dair kohr-res-pon-dent) – correspondent (male)

- **die Korrespondentin** (pronounced: dee kohr-res-pon-den-tin) – correspondent (female)

Here are some sentences using these words:

- **Die Sendung beginnt um sieben Uhr.** (pronounced: dee zen-doong beh-ginnt oom zee-ben oor) – The show begins at seven o'clock.

- **Er arbeitet als Korrespondent für die Zeitung.** (pronounced: air ar-bai-tet ahls kohr-res-pon-dent fuer dee tsai-toong) – He works as a correspondent for the newspaper.

- **Wir schauen den Kanal für Nachrichten.** (pronounced: veer shou-en den kah-nahl fuer nah-rikh-ten) – We watch the channel for news.

These examples will help you use broadcasting and journalism vocabulary in German.

Advertising and Marketing Vocabulary

Advertising and marketing are ways to promote products and services. Here are some German words related to advertising and marketing:

- **die Werbung** (pronounced: dee vair-boong) – advertisement

- **die Anzeige** (pronounced: dee ahn-tsigh-eh) – ad, notice

- **die Marke** (pronounced: dee mar-keh) – brand

- **das Plakat** (pronounced: das plah-kaht) – poster

- **der Slogan** (pronounced: dair sloh-gahn) – slogan

- **die Kampagne** (pronounced: dee kahm-pahn-yeh) – campaign

Here are some example sentences:

- **Die Werbung ist sehr kreativ.** (pronounced: dee vair-boong ist zair kreh-ah-teef) – The advertisement is very creative.

- **Wir machen eine neue Kampagne für die Marke.** (pronounced: veer mah-khen eye-neh noy-eh kahm-pahn-yeh fuer dee mar-keh) – We are doing a new campaign for the brand.

- **Das Plakat hängt an der Wand.** (pronounced: das plah-kaht hengt an dair vahnd) – The poster is hanging on the wall.

These sentences help you understand how to use advertising and marketing words.

Useful Phrases for Media and Communications

Here are some useful phrases that will help you talk about media and communications in German:

- **Welche Sendung schaust du gern?** (pronounced: vel-khe zen-doong shoust doo gairn) – Which show do you like to watch?

- **Kann ich eine E-Mail senden?** (pronounced: kann ikh eye-neh ee-mail zen-den) – Can I send an email?

- **Was sind die neuesten Nachrichten?** (pronounced: vas zint dee noy-es-ten nah-rikh-ten) – What is the latest news?

These phrases will help you engage in conversations about media and communications topics in German.

Key Points to Remember

- **Basic Media Words:** Learn words like "Zeitung" (newspaper) and "Fernsehen" (television) to talk about different types of media.

- **Digital Media Terms:** Use words like "Internet" (internet) and "E-Mail" (email) to discuss online communication.

- **Communication Tools:** Know words like "Telefon" (telephone) and "Kamera" (camera) to talk about communication tools.

- **Broadcasting and Journalism:** Use terms like "Sendung" (show) and "Journalist" (journalist) for media discussions.

- **Advertising and Marketing:** Understand terms like "Werbung" (advertisement) and "Marke" (brand) to talk about promotions.

Chapter 41

Advanced Conversation Topics

Now that you have learned the basics of the German language, it's time to explore some advanced conversation topics. These topics will help you engage in deeper conversations with others and express your thoughts and opinions more clearly. In this chapter, we will learn some important phrases and vocabulary that can help you discuss topics like hobbies, school, family, future plans, and current events in German. Let's start by exploring how to talk about hobbies and interests!

Talking About Hobbies and Interests

When you meet new people, a great way to start a conversation is by talking about hobbies and interests. Here are some phrases to help you talk about your favorite activities:

- **Was machst du gern in deiner Freizeit?** (pronounced: vas makhst doo gairn in digh-ner fry-tsite) – What do you like to do in your free time?
- **Ich spiele gern Fußball.** (pronounced: ikh shpee-leh gairn foos-ball) – I like to play soccer.
- **Sie liest gern Bücher.** (pronounced: zee leest gairn bew-kher) – She likes to read books.
- **Wir hören gern Musik.** (pronounced: veer hoer-en gairn moo-zeek) – We like to listen to music.

You can also ask others about their interests:

- **Hast du ein Hobby?** (pronounced: hahst doo ine hoh-bee) – Do you have a hobby?
- **Welcher Sport gefällt dir?** (pronounced: vel-kher shport geh-felt deer) – Which sport do you like?

These phrases will help you start a friendly conversation about hobbies and interests.

Discussing School and Learning

Another common topic is school and learning. Here are some useful phrases to talk about your school experience in German:

- **Wie heißt deine Schule?** (pronounced: vee highst digh-neh shoo-leh) – What is your school called?

- **Ich gehe in die sechste Klasse.** (pronounced: ikh geh-heh in dee zekh-steh klas-seh) – I am in the sixth grade.

- **Mein Lieblingsfach ist Mathematik.** (pronounced: mine lee-blingz-fakh ist mah-teh-mah-teek) – My favorite subject is math.

- **Welche Fächer magst du?** (pronounced: vel-khe feh-kher mahkst doo) – Which subjects do you like?

To ask someone about their studies, you can use these phrases:

- **Was lernst du in der Schule?** (pronounced: vas ler-nst doo in dair shoo-leh) – What do you learn in school?

- **Findest du Geschichte interessant?** (pronounced: fin-dest doo ge-shikh-teh in-te-res-sahnt) – Do you find history interesting?

These sentences will help you talk about school and learning with your friends and classmates.

Talking About Family

Family is an important topic in many conversations. Here are some phrases to help you talk about your family in German:

- **Hast du Geschwister?** (pronounced: hahst doo ge-shvist-er) – Do you have siblings?

- **Ich habe einen Bruder und eine Schwester.** (pronounced: ikh hah-beh eye-nen broo-der oond eye-neh shvest-er) – I have a brother and a sister.

- **Meine Eltern sind sehr nett.** (pronounced: mine el-tern zint zair nett) – My parents are very nice.

- **Wie alt sind deine Großeltern?** (pronounced: vee ahlt zind digh-neh grohs-el-tern) – How old are your grandparents?

You can also ask about someone else's family:

- **Wer ist in deiner Familie?** (pronounced: vair ist in digh-ner fah-mee-lee-eh) – Who is in your family?

- **Wo wohnen deine Verwandten?** (pronounced: voh voh-nen digh-neh fer-vant-ten) – Where do your relatives live?

These phrases will help you share information about your family and ask about others.

Discussing Future Plans

Talking about the future is another interesting conversation topic. Here are some phrases to help you discuss future plans in German:

- **Was möchtest du in der Zukunft machen?** (pronounced: vas merkh-test doo in dair tsoo-koonft mah-khen) – What would you like to do in the future?

- **Ich möchte Arzt werden.** (pronounced: ikh merkh-teh artsd vair-den) – I want to become a doctor.

- **Wir planen eine Reise nach Europa.** (pronounced: veer plah-nen eye-neh ry-zeh nahkh oy-roh-pah) – We are planning a trip to Europe.

- **Hast du Pläne für die Sommerferien?** (pronounced: hahst doo pleh-neh fuer dee zom-mer-feh-ree-en) – Do you have plans for the summer holidays?

You can also ask about someone's dreams or ambitions:

- **Was ist dein Traumjob?** (pronounced: vas ist dine troum-yob) – What is your dream job?

- **Wo möchtest du in zehn Jahren sein?** (pronounced: voh merkh-test doo in tsehn yah-ren zine) – Where do you want to be in ten years?

These sentences will help you talk about future plans and dreams in German.

Talking About Current Events

Discussing current events is a great way to have meaningful conversations. Here are some useful phrases to talk about news and events in German:

- **Hast du die Nachrichten gesehen?** (pronounced: hahst doo dee nah-rikh-ten geh-zeh-en) – Did you see the news?

- **Was denkst du über den Klimawandel?** (pronounced: vas denkst doo oo-ber den klee-mah-vahn-del) – What do you think about climate change?

- **Ich finde das Thema sehr wichtig.** (pronounced: ikh fin-deh das teh-mah zair vik-tikh) – I find this topic very important.

- **Wir haben über Politik gesprochen.** (pronounced: veer hah-ben oo-ber poh-lee-teek gesh-pro-khen) – We talked about politics.

To ask for someone's opinion, use these phrases:

- **Was ist deine Meinung dazu?** (pronounced: vas ist digh-neh my-noong dah-tsoo) – What is your opinion on this?

- **Interessierst du dich für die Umwelt?** (pronounced: in-te-res-see-erst doo dikh fuer dee oom-velt) – Are you interested in the environment?

These phrases will help you talk about important topics and share opinions.

Expressing Feelings and Opinions

It's also useful to know how to express your feelings and opinions in German. Here are some common phrases:

- **Ich finde das toll!** (pronounced: ikh fin-deh das toll) – I think that's great!

- **Das gefällt mir nicht.** (pronounced: das geh-felt meer nisht) – I don't like that.

- **Ich bin froh darüber.** (pronounced: ikh bin froh dah-roo-ber) – I am happy about that.

- **Das macht mich traurig.** (pronounced: das makht mikh trou-rikh) – That makes me sad.

To ask how someone feels, use these phrases:

- **Wie fühlst du dich?** (pronounced: vee fuehlst doo dikh) – How do you feel?

- **Bist du zufrieden?** (pronounced: bist doo tsoo-free-den) – Are you satisfied?

These expressions will help you share your feelings and opinions in conversations.

Key Points to Remember

- **Hobbies and Interests:** Use phrases like "Was machst du gern?" to talk about what you like to do.

- **School and Learning:** Discuss school topics using sentences like "Ich gehe in die sechste Klasse."

- **Family Talk:** Share family details with phrases like "Hast du Geschwister?"

- **Future Plans:** Express future goals with questions like "Was möchtest du in der Zukunft machen?"

- **Current Events:** Talk about news and opinions with phrases like "Hast du die Nachrichten gesehen?"

Chapter 42

Translation Techniques

Translation is the process of changing words and sentences from one language into another. When learning German, understanding translation techniques can help you better grasp how sentences are formed and how words are used in different contexts. In this chapter, we will learn some simple techniques for translating from German to English and vice versa. This will help you improve your understanding and make it easier to communicate with others in both languages.

Understanding Word-for-Word Translation

The simplest way to start translating is by using a word-for-word approach. This means you translate each word individually from one language to another. For example:

- **German:** Ich bin müde.
  Word-for-word Translation: I am tired.

- **German:** Der Hund ist groß.
  Word-for-word Translation: The dog is big.

While this technique is straightforward, it doesn't always work perfectly because German and English have different grammar rules. Sometimes, a word-for-word translation might not make sense or sound natural. For example:

- **German:** Ich habe Hunger.
  Word-for-word Translation: I have hunger.
  Better Translation: I am hungry.

Here, you can see that while the literal translation is "I have hunger," the better translation in English is "I am hungry." This is why understanding context and grammar is important when translating.

Understanding Context in Translation

Context means understanding the situation in which words are used. The same word can have different meanings depending on where and how it is used. Let's look at an example:

- **German:** Bank
  Possible Translations: bank (as in a financial institution) or bench (a place to sit)

To figure out which meaning is correct, you need to look at the context of the sentence:

- **German:** Ich gehe zur Bank. (pronounced: ikh geh-heh tsoor bank)
  Translation: I am going to the bank. (Here, "Bank" means the financial institution.)

- **German:** Ich sitze auf der Bank. (pronounced: ikh sit-zeh owf dair bank)
  Translation: I am sitting on the bench. (Here, "Bank" means a bench.)

Understanding the context helps you choose the right translation and makes sure that the meaning is clear.

Learning Common Phrases and Idioms

Some phrases in German do not translate directly into English because they are idioms, which means they have a special meaning that isn't obvious from the individual words. Learning common phrases and idioms can help you become a better translator. Here are a few examples:

- **German:** Tomaten auf den Augen haben. (pronounced: toh-mah-ten owf den ow-gen hah-ben)
  Literal Translation: To have tomatoes on the eyes.
  Actual Meaning: To be oblivious to something.

- **German:** Ich drücke dir die Daumen. (pronounced: ikh druek-keh deer dee dow-men)
  Literal Translation: I press my thumbs for you.
  Actual Meaning: I am keeping my fingers crossed for you.

Knowing idioms and common phrases helps you translate in a way that captures the true meaning rather than just the words themselves.

Understanding Sentence Structure

German and English have different rules for how sentences are formed. Understanding these differences can help you translate more accurately. Here are some key points:

- **Word Order:** In German, the verb often comes second in a sentence, while in English, it can vary. For example:
  German: Ich lerne Deutsch. (pronounced: ikh layr-neh doytsh)
  Translation: I learn German.

- **Questions:** In German, questions are often formed by placing the verb first:
  German: Kannst du mir helfen? (pronounced: kahnst doo meer hel-fen)
  Translation: Can you help me?

Understanding these differences will help you translate sentences correctly and make them sound natural in English.

Using Synonyms to Improve Translation

Sometimes, there isn't a direct translation for a word from German to English. In these cases, you can use a synonym, which is a word with a similar meaning. For example:

- **German:** Der Film ist spannend. (pronounced: dair film ist shpan-nend)
  Direct Translation: The film is exciting.
  Synonym Translation: The film is thrilling.

Using synonyms helps you find the right word to express the same idea in English.

Translating Expressions of Time

Translating time expressions can also be challenging because German uses specific words f or different times of the day. Here are some examples:

- **German:** am Morgen (pronounced: am mor-gen) – in the morning

- **German:** am Nachmittag (pronounced: am nakh-mit-tahk) – in the afternoon

- **German:** um Mitternacht (pronounced: oom mit-ter-nakht) – at midnight

When translating, make sure you use the correct English phrase that matches the time expression in German.

Using Online Tools and Dictionaries

Online tools and dictionaries can be very helpful when translating. They can provide translations for words, phrases, and sentences, and help you understand different meanings. However, it's important to remember that these tools are not always perfect, so always double-check the context and grammar.

- Use a **German-English dictionary** to look up words you don't know.

- Use **translation apps** to get a quick translation, but remember to review the translation to make sure it makes sense.

- Ask a teacher or native speaker if you are unsure about a translation.

These tools are great resources for helping you learn and improve your translation skills.

Practice Makes Perfect

The best way to get better at translating is by practicing regularly. Here are some activities to help you practice:

- **Translate Simple Sentences:** Start with easy sentences and translate them from German to English and back.

- **Read Bilingual Books:** Read books that have both German and English text side by side.

- **Watch German Videos with English Subtitles:** This helps you see how German words and phrases are translated into English.

Practicing translation regularly will help you become more confident and accurate over time.

Key Points to Remember

- **Word-for-Word Translation:** Start by translating each word, but remember that sometimes a direct translation does not always make sense.

- **Understand Context:** Look at the whole sentence to understand the meaning before translating.

- **Learn Common Phrases:** Memorize common idioms and phrases that don't translate directly.

- **Use Synonyms:** Find similar words in English to better express the meaning.

- **Practice Regularly:** Use tools, read, and translate often to improve your skills.

Chapter 43

Interpreting Techniques

Interpreting is different from translating. While translating involves changing written text from one language to another, interpreting is all about listening to someone speaking in one language and saying it in another language right away. It's like being a bridge between two people who speak different languages. In this chapter, we will learn some basic techniques for interpreting from German to English and vice versa. These techniques will help you understand and convey the right meaning when people are speaking in German.

Listening Carefully

The first and most important step in interpreting is listening carefully. You need to understand what the person is saying before you can interpret it. Here are some tips to help you listen better:

- **Focus on Key Words:** Pay attention to the main words that convey the message. For example, if someone says, "Ich habe Durst" (pronounced: ikh hah-beh doorst), the key word is "Durst," which means "thirst." This helps you know they are talking about being thirsty.

- **Listen for Context:** Try to understand the situation. If you know what the conversation is about, it will help you make sense of the words. For example, if the conversation is happening at a restaurant, words like Essen (food) or Getränk (drink) might be common.

- **Stay Calm:** Don't panic if you don't understand every word. Focus on the overall meaning of the sentence. Often, understanding the general idea is more important than knowing every single word.

By practicing careful listening, you will get better at understanding spoken German and interpreting it correctly.

Understanding the Difference Between Literal and Meaningful Interpretation

When interpreting, it is important to capture the true meaning of what is being said, not just the words. Sometimes a word-for-word interpretation does not make sense. Here is an example:

- **German:** Ich drücke dir die Daumen. (pronounced: ikh druek-keh deer dee dow-men)
  Literal Interpretation: I press my thumbs for you.
  Meaningful Interpretation: I am keeping my fingers crossed for you.

In this example, the literal interpretation does not make sense in English, but the meaningful interpretation does. Always try to convey the real meaning behind the words.

Interpreting with Gestures and Expressions

Sometimes, people use gestures and facial expressions to help communicate their message. As an interpreter, you should pay attention to these non-verbal clues. They can give you more information about what the person is trying to say. Here are some examples:

- If someone smiles and says, "Das ist wunderbar!" (pronounced: das ist voon-der-bahr), their smile shows they are happy or pleased. You can interpret it as, "That is wonderful!"

- If someone frowns and says, "Das gefällt mir nicht." (pronounced: das geh-felt meer nisht), their frown shows they are unhappy or dissatisfied. You can interpret it as, "I d on't like that."

Gestures and expressions help you understand how someone feels, making your interpretation more accurate.

Breaking Down Long Sentences

When someone speaks in long sentences, it can be challenging to interpret everything at once. Here are some techniques to help you break down long sentences:

- **Pause and Chunk:** Listen to a few words or a part of the sentence, then interpret that part before moving to the next. For example, if someone says, "Ich möchte ein großes Eis, weil es so heiß ist." (pronounced: ikh merkh-teh ine groh-ses ice, veyl es zo hise ist), you can break it down into: "I would like a big ice cream," (pause) "because it is so hot."

- **Look for Connectors:** Words like und (and), aber (but), and weil (because) are connectors. Use these words to help you split the sentence into smaller parts that are easier to interpret.

Breaking down long sentences into smaller chunks makes it easier to remember and interpret them accurately.

Staying Neutral and Clear

As an interpreter, it is important to stay neutral and clear. This means you should not add your own opinions or emotions to the interpretation. Here are some tips to help you stay neutral:

- **Use the Same Tone:** If the person speaking is calm, interpret calmly. If they are excited, use an excited tone. This helps keep the interpretation true to the speaker's intent.

- **Be Accurate:** Don't change the meaning of what is being said. If someone says, "Ich bin traurig." (pronounced: ikh bin trou-rikh), which means "I am sad," don't interpret it as "I am unhappy." Instead, keep the original word "sad" to stay accurate.

Being neutral and clear helps ensure that your interpretation is reliable and trustworthy.

Using Simplified Language

Sometimes, it is helpful to use simpler words when interpreting, especially if the person you are interpreting for is young or learning the language. Here are some ways to simplify language:

- **Use Basic Words:** Instead of using complex vocabulary, use simple words. For example, instead of saying, "kompliziert" (pronounced: kom-pli-tseert), which means "complicated," you can use "schwierig" (pronounced: shveer-ikh), which means "difficult."

- **Avoid Idioms:** Idioms can be confusing because they don't always make sense literally. Try to use straightforward language that is easy to understand.

Using simplified language makes it easier for everyone to understand the interpretation.

Asking for Clarification

Sometimes, you might not understand what someone is saying, or you might not be sure of the correct interpretation. In these cases, it is okay to ask for clarification. Here are some ways to do that:

- **Repeat the Question:** If you didn't hear or understand something, you can say, "Können Sie das bitte wiederholen?" (pronounced: koe-nen zee das bit-teh vee-der-ho-len) – Can you please repeat that?

- **Ask for Meaning:** If you are unsure about a word, you can ask, "Was bedeutet das?" (pronounced: vas beh-doy-tet das) – What does that mean?

Asking for clarification ensures that your interpretation is accurate and that you understand the message correctly.

Practice and Improve Your Skills

The more you practice interpreting, the better you will become. Here are some ways to practice:

- **Practice with Friends:** Find a friend who speaks German and practice interpreting conversations together.

- **Listen to German Audio:** Listen to German audio clips or videos and try to interpret them into English.

- **Use Language Apps:** Many apps offer interpreting exercises that can help you improve your skills.

Regular practice will help you become a more confident and skilled interpreter.

Key Points to Remember

- **Listen Carefully:** Focus on key words, understand context, and stay calm to interpret accurately.

- **Capture the Meaning:** Convey the true meaning behind the words, not just the literal translation.

- **Use Non-Verbal Cues:** Pay attention to gestures and facial expressions to better understand the message.

- **Ask for Clarification:** Don't hesitate to ask questions if you are unsure about what is being said.

- **Practice Regularly:** The more you practice, the more confident and accurate you will become.

Chapter 44

German Dialects and Regional Variations

German is spoken in many different regions, and each region has its own way of speaking the language. These different ways of speaking are called dialects. A dialect is a variation of a language that includes unique words, pronunciations, and expressions that are different from the standard form of the language. In Germany, there are many dialects, and each one has its special characteristics. In this chapter, we will learn about some of the main German dialects, where they are spoken, and how they differ from each other. This will help you understand why German can sound different in different parts of the country.

What is High German (Hochdeutsch)?

Before we learn about the different dialects, it's important to know about "High German" or Hochdeutsch (pronounced: hohk-doitsh). High German is the standard form of the German language. It is used in schools, books, newspapers, and television. When people from different parts of Germany talk to each other, they usually use High German because it is understood by everyone. Think of High German like standard English – it's the version everyone learns, no matter where they live.

Different Regions, Different Dialects

Germany is divided into many regions, and each has its own dialect. Let's look at some of the most common ones:

Bavarian Dialect (Bairisch)

The Bavarian dialect, or Bairisch (pronounced: bye-rish), is spoken in Bavaria, a region in the southeast of Germany. Bavarian is known for its unique pronunciation and words. Here are some examples:

- **German:** Guten Morgen (Good morning)
  Bavarian: Grüß Gott (pronounced: gruess got)

- **German:** Danke (Thank you)
  Bavarian: Vergelt's Gott (pronounced: fair-gelts got)

- **German:** Ja (Yes)
  Bavarian: Jo (pronounced: yo)

Bavarian is a fun dialect that can sound quite different from High German. People in Bavaria use many words that are not used in other parts of Germany.

Berlin Dialect (Berlinerisch)

The Berlin dialect, or Berlinerisch (pronounced: ber-leen-er-ish), is spoken in the capital city, Berlin. This dialect has its own special flavor, with some unique words and expressions:

- **German:** Kartoffeln (Potatoes)
  Berlin Dialect: Knollen (pronounced: knoll-en)

- **German:** Polizist (Policeman)
  Berlin Dialect: Bulle (pronounced: bool-leh)

- **German:** Kind (Child)
  Berlin Dialect: Göre (pronounced: ger-reh)

Berliners are known for their humor and often use playful language. The Berlin dialect sounds a bit rough but is full of character!

Swabian Dialect (Schwäbisch)

The Swabian dialect, or Schwäbisch (pronounced: shway-bish), is spoken in the southwest of Germany, mainly in the region of Baden-Württemberg. This dialect has a unique melody, and here are some examples:

- **German:** Hallo (Hello)
  Swabian: Grüß di (pronounced: gruess dee)

- **German:** Freund (Friend)
  Swabian: Fehl (pronounced: feh-leh)

- **German:** Kleine (Small)

Swabian: Koin (pronounced: koin)

Swabian sounds very different from other German dialects, and sometimes it can be hard to understand even for native German speakers!

Saxon Dialect (Sächsisch)

The Saxon dialect, or Sächsisch (pronounced: zek-sish), is spoken in the eastern part of Germany, mainly in the state of Saxony. This dialect has some distinct sounds and words:

- **German:** Ich (I)
  Saxon: Isch (pronounced: ish)

- **German:** Entschuldigung (Sorry)
  Saxon: Schuldijung (pronounced: shool-dee-yung)

- **German:** Gut (Good)
  Saxon: Guud (pronounced: goot)

The Saxon dialect is known for its soft sounds and unique pronunciation. It often sounds like a mix between High German and other regional dialects.

Why Are There So Many Dialects?

Germany has many dialects because the country is made up of many different regions with their own cultures, histories, and ways of speaking. Over time, these regions developed their own unique versions of German. People in each area would use words and expressions that were influenced by their surroundings, local traditions, and even other languages.

For example, the Bavarian dialect has been influenced by Austria, while the Saxon dialect has been influenced by Slavic languages. This is why German sounds different in different parts of the country.

How to Understand Different Dialects

If you are learning German, it's important to start with High German, as it is the standard form used everywhere. However, it can be fun to learn a few words and phrases from different dialects! Here are some tips to help you understand different dialects:

- **Watch Local Shows:** Watching TV shows or movies from different regions can help you hear how people speak in those areas.

- **Listen to Music:** Many songs are sung in different dialects, and listening to them can help you get used to the sounds.

- **Talk to Native Speakers:** If you meet someone from Germany, ask them to teach you some words from their dialect. They might enjoy sharing their unique way of speaking with you!

Learning about different dialects can help you better understand the culture and diversity of Germany.

Key Points to Remember

- **High German (Hochdeutsch):** The standard form of German used in schools, books, and media.

- **Different Regions, Different Dialects:** Each region in Germany has its own dialect with unique words and pronunciations.

- **Bavarian, Berlin, Swabian, and Saxon Dialects:** These are just a few examples of the many German dialects, each with its own special characteristics.

- **Dialects Reflect History and Culture:** Dialects have developed over time due to regional influences and traditions.

- **Start with High German:** Learning High German first is important, but exploring dialects can be a fun way to learn more about German culture.

Chapter 45

Professional Language Use

When people work in a professional setting, like an office, school, or business, they often use a different style of language than when they are speaking with friends or family. This type of language is called "professional language." Professional language is more formal and polite. It shows respect and makes communication clear and effective. In this chapter, we will learn how to use professional language in German, including some useful phrases and words that are often used in professional settings. This will help you understand how to speak politely and appropriately in different situations.

Using Formal Greetings and Introductions

When meeting someone in a professional setting, it is important to use formal greetings. Here are some examples of how to greet people formally in German:

- **German:** Guten Morgen (pronounced: goo-ten mor-gen) – Good morning
- **German:** Guten Tag (pronounced: goo-ten tahk) – Good day
- **German:** Guten Abend (pronounced: goo-ten ah-bent) – Good evening

When introducing yourself in a professional environment, you should use polite phrases:

- **German:** Mein Name ist… (pronounced: mine nah-meh ist) – My name is…
- **German:** Es freut mich, Sie kennenzulernen. (pronounced: es froyt mikh, zee ken-nen-tsoo-lair-nen) – I am pleased to meet you.

Using these formal greetings and introductions shows respect and professionalism.

Polite Forms of Address

In German, there are two ways to say "you": du (pronounced: doo) and Sie (pronounced: zee). In professional settings, it is more polite to use Sie when speaking to someone you do not know well or someone in a higher position.

Here are some examples:

- **German:** Können Sie mir helfen? (pronounced: koe-nen zee meer hel-fen) – Can you help me?
- **German:** Haben Sie einen Moment Zeit? (pronounced: hah-ben zee eye-nen moh-ment tsight) – Do you have a moment?

Always use Sie in professional settings unless the person tells you that it is okay to use du.

Expressing Politeness with "Bitte" and "Danke"

Politeness is very important in professional settings. Words like "please" and "thank you" are used often to show respect. Here are the German words for these polite expressions:

- **German:** Bitte (pronounced: bit-teh) – Please
- **German:** Danke (pronounced: dank-eh) – Thank you

Here are some examples of how to use these words in sentences:

- **German:** Könnten Sie mir bitte die Datei schicken? (pronounced: koent-ten zee meer bit-teh dee dah-tye shik-ken) – Could you please send me the file?
- **German:** Vielen Dank für Ihre Hilfe. (pronounced: fee-len dank fuer ee-reh hil-feh) – Thank you very much for your help.

Using Bitte and Danke frequently shows that you are polite and respectful.

Making Requests and Giving Instructions

In professional settings, you often need to make requests or give instructions. Here are some useful phrases in German for these situations:

- **German:** Könnten Sie das bitte erklären? (pronounced: koen-ten zee das bit-teh ek-lair-en) – Could you please explain that?

- **German:** Würden Sie mir bitte die Unterlagen senden? (pronounced: voord-en zee meer bit-teh dee oon-ter-lah-gen zen-den) – Would you please send me the documents?

- **German:** Bitte nehmen Sie Platz. (pronounced: bit-teh nay-men zee plats) – Please take a seat.

These phrases help you communicate requests or instructions in a polite and professional manner.

Apologizing and Correcting Mistakes

In any professional environment, mistakes can happen. When they do, it's important to apologize politely. Here are some phrases for apologizing and addressing mistakes in German:

- **German:** Entschuldigen Sie bitte. (pronounced: ent-shool-dee-gen zee bit-teh) – I am sorry.

- **German:** Es tut mir leid. (pronounced: es toot meer lite) – I apologize.

- **German:** Können wir das korrigieren? (pronounced: koe-nen veer das koh-ree-geer-en) – Can we correct this?

Being able to apologize and offer solutions shows professionalism and maturity.

Ending Conversations Politely

Ending conversations politely is as important as starting them. Here are some common phrases to close a conversation in a professional setting:

- **German:** Vielen Dank für Ihre Zeit. (pronounced: fee-len dank fuer ee-reh tsight) – Thank you for your time.

- **German:** Ich freue mich auf unsere Zusammenarbeit. (pronounced: ikh fro-yeh mikh owf oon-seh-reh tsoo-sah-men-ar-bite) – I look forward to our cooperation.

- **German:** Auf Wiedersehen. (pronounced: owf vee-der-zay-en) – Goodbye.

Using these phrases shows that you value the conversation and are respectful to the person you are speaking with.

Common Professional Titles and Positions

In a professional environment, people often address each other by their titles or positions. Here are some common titles in German:

- **Herr** (pronounced: hair) – Mr.

- **Frau** (pronounced: frow) – Mrs. or Ms.

- **Doktor** (pronounced: dok-tor) – Doctor

- **Professor** (pronounced: pro-fes-sor) – Professor

- **Direktor** (pronounced: dee-rek-tor) – Director

Using these titles correctly is a sign of respect and is important in professional language use.

Writing Professional Emails

In professional settings, emails are a common way to communicate. Here are some useful phrases for writing professional emails in German:

- **German:** Sehr geehrte Damen und Herren, (pronounced: zair ge-air-teh dah-men oond hair-ren) – Dear Sir or Madam,

- **German:** Mit freundlichen Grüßen, (pronounced: mit froind-likh-en grue-sen) – Sincerely,

- **German:** Ich freue mich auf Ihre Antwort. (pronounced: ikh fro-yeh mikh owf ee-reh ant-vort) – I look forward to your response.

Using polite and professional language in emails helps make a good impression and shows respect.

Key Points to Remember

- **Use Formal Greetings:** Start conversations with phrases like "Guten Morgen" or "Guten Tag" in professional settings.

- **Address People Politely:** Use Sie instead of du when speaking to someone formally.

- **Be Polite with Words Like "Bitte" and "Danke":** Use these words often to show respect.

- **Use Professional Titles:** Address people by their correct titles, like Herr, Frau, or Doktor.

- **Write Professional Emails:** Use polite phrases to make a good impression in written communication.

Chapter 46

Traveling, Living, and Working in Germany

If you ever think about visiting Germany, living there for a while, or even working there, it's good to know some important things about daily life in Germany. This chapter will help you understand what to expect and how to communicate while traveling, living, or working in Germany. We will learn useful phrases, cultural tips, and practical information to help you feel comfortable in this new environment.

Getting Around in Germany

Germany has a great transportation system, which makes it easy to travel around the country. Here are some common ways people get around in Germany:

- **Die Bahn** (pronounced: dee bahn) – The train. Germany has many fast trains, like the ICE (InterCity Express), which connects major cities.

- **Die U-Bahn** (pronounced: dee oo-bahn) – The subway. This is used mainly in big cities like Berlin, Munich, and Hamburg.

- **Der Bus** (pronounced: dair boos) – The bus. Buses are used for local travel and can take you to places the trains or subways don't reach.

- **Das Taxi** (pronounced: das tak-see) – The taxi. Taxis are available in most cities, but they are usually more expensive than public transport.

If you want to buy a ticket for the train or bus, you can use these phrases:

- **German:** Wo kann ich ein Ticket kaufen? (pronounced: voh kahn ikh ine tik-et kau-fen) – Where can I buy a ticket?

- **German:** Wie viel kostet ein Ticket nach Berlin? (pronounced: vee feel kohs-tet ine tik-et nahkh bair-leen) – How much does a ticket to Berlin cost?

Using these phrases will help you navigate the transportation system in Germany easily.

Finding a Place to Live

If you plan to stay in Germany for a while, you will need a place to live. Here are some common types of housing in Germany:

- **Die Wohnung** (pronounced: dee voh-noong) – The apartment. Apartments are common in German cities, and you can find both small and large ones.

- **Das Haus** (pronounced: das hous) – The house. If you prefer more space, you might look for a house, especially in smaller towns or rural areas.

- **Das Studentenwohnheim** (pronounced: das shtoo-den-ten-vohn-hime) – The student dormitory. These are great for students who are studying in Germany.

When looking for a place to live, here are some useful phrases:

- **German:** Gibt es freie Wohnungen? (pronounced: gibt es fry-eh voh-noong-en) – Are there any available apartments?

- **German:** Wie hoch ist die Miete? (pronounced: vee hohk ist dee mee-teh) – How much is the rent?

These phrases will help you ask about housing options and find a comfortable place to stay.

Everyday Life in Germany

Living in Germany can be a fun experience. Let's learn some common phrases and words you might need in your daily life:

- **German:** Wo ist der Supermarkt? (pronounced: voh ist dair soo-per-mahrkt) – Where is the supermarket?

- **German:** Ich brauche Brot und Milch. (pronounced: ikh brow-khe broht oond milkh) – I need bread and milk.

- **German:** Wie spät ist es? (pronounced: vee shpaet ist es) – What time is it?

- **German:** Kann ich mit Karte zahlen? (pronounced: kahn ikh mit kar-teh tsah-len) – Can I pay with a card?

These sentences will help you communicate in stores, at the market, or when asking for help.

Understanding German Culture

Germany has its own culture and traditions. Here are a few things to keep in mind:

- **Punctuality:** Germans are known for being on time. If you have an appointment, be sure to arrive a few minutes early or exactly on time.

- **Recycling:** Germans take recycling very seriously. You will see different bins for different types of waste – make sure to put your trash in the correct bin!

- **Politeness:** Use polite words like Bitte (please) and Danke (thank you) often. This shows respect and helps you make a good impression.

Knowing these cultural tips will help you fit in and feel comfortable in Germany.

Working in Germany

If you decide to work in Germany, it's good to know some important phrases and words for the workplace. Here are a few examples:

- **Die Arbeit** (pronounced: dee ar-bite) – The work or job

- **Der Chef** (pronounced: dair shef) – The boss

- **Die Kollegen** (pronounced: dee koh-lay-gen) – The colleagues

- **Das Büro** (pronounced: das byu-roh) – The office

Here are some useful phrases for working in a German environment:

- **German:** Ich bin neu hier. (pronounced: ikh bin noy heer) – I am new here.

- **German:** Könnten Sie mir helfen? (pronounced: koen-ten zee meer hel-fen) – Could you help me?

- **German:** Wann ist das Meeting? (pronounced: vahn ist das mee-ting) – When is the meeting?

Using these phrases will help you communicate with your colleagues and get comfortable in your new job.

Exploring Germany

Germany is full of interesting places to explore! Here are some famous cities and what you can find there:

- **Berlin:** The capital city, known for its history, museums, and the Brandenburg Gate.
- **Munich (München):** Famous for Oktoberfest, beautiful parks, and old buildings.
- **Hamburg:** A port city known for its harbor and delicious seafood.
- **Frankfurt:** A financial hub with modern skyscrapers and a historic old town.

When exploring Germany, you might find these phrases useful:

- **German:** Wo ist das Museum? (pronounced: voh ist das moo-zay-oom) – Where is the museum?
- **German:** Wie komme ich zum Park? (pronounced: vee koh-meh ikh tsoom park) – How do I get to the park?

Exploring new places in Germany is a great way to learn about the country's history and culture.

Enjoying Local Food

Germany has delicious food to try! Here are some common dishes you might find:

- **Das Brötchen** (pronounced: das broet-chen) – A small bread roll, often eaten for breakfast.
- **Die Wurst** (pronounced: dee voorst) – Sausage, which is very popular in Germany .
- **Der Apfelstrudel** (pronounced: dair ap-fel-stroo-del) – Apple strudel, a sweet dessert made with apples.

To order food, you can use these phrases:

- **German:** Ich möchte ein Brötchen, bitte. (pronounced: ikh merkh-teh ine broet-chen, bit-teh) – I would like a bread roll, please.
- **German:** Haben Sie eine Speisekarte auf Englisch? (pronounced: hah-ben zee eye-neh shpy-zeh-kar-teh owf eng-lish) – Do you have a menu in English?

Trying local food is a fun way to experience German culture!

Key Points to Remember

- **Use Public Transport:** Learn words like "die Bahn" (the train) to navigate Germany's transport system.

- **Find a Place to Live:** Ask about housing using phrases like "Gibt es freie Wohnungen?"

- **Learn About the Culture:** Remember cultural tips, like being on time and recycling.

- **Work Professionally:** Use phrases like "Ich bin neu hier" to communicate in the workplace.

- **Explore and Enjoy:** Try local food and explore cities like Berlin and Munich to fully enjoy your time in Germany.

Chapter 47

Final Review and Assessment

Congratulations! You have reached the final chapter of this book. By now, you have learned many important aspects of the German language, including basic vocabulary, grammar, useful phrases, and cultural tips. In this chapter, we will review what you have learned so far and give you some exercises to help you assess your understanding. This will help you see how much progress you've made and where you might need a little more practice.

Review of Key Vocabulary

Let's start by reviewing some of the essential German words and phrases you've learned throughout the book. These words will help you communicate in various situations:

- **Basic Greetings:** Hallo (pronounced: hah-loh) – Hello, Guten Morgen (pronounced: goo-ten mor-gen) – Good morning.

- **Polite Words:** Bitte (pronounced: bit-teh) – Please, Danke (pronounced: dank-eh) – Thank you.

- **Common Phrases:** Wie geht es Ihnen? (pronounced: vee geht es een-en) – How are you?, Ich verstehe nicht (pronounced: ikh fer-shtay-eh nikht) – I don't understand.

- **Numbers:** Eins (pronounced: ayns) – One, Zwei (pronounced: tsvigh) – Two, Drei (pronounced: dri) – Three.

- **Days of the Week:** Montag (pronounced: mohn-tahg) – Monday, Dienstag (pronounced: deens-tahg) – Tuesday.

Try to remember these key words and phrases as they are essential for everyday conversations in German.

Review of Grammar Points

Grammar is the foundation of any language, and you've learned some important rules for German grammar. Let's review a few key points:

- **Nouns and Articles:** In German, all nouns have a gender: masculine (der), feminine (die), or neuter (das). For example, der Hund (pronounced: dair hoond) – the dog (masculine), die Katze (pronounced: dee kaht-zeh) – the cat (feminine), das Haus (pronounced: das hous) – the house (neuter).

- **Basic Verb Conjugation:** You learned how to conjugate regular verbs like spielen (to play): ich spiele (I play), du spielst (you play), er/sie/es spielt (he/she/it plays).

- **Present Tense:** The present tense is used to talk about actions happening now. For example, Ich lerne Deutsch (pronounced: ikh layr-neh doytsh) – I am learning German.

- **Question Words:** Words like wer (who), was (what), wo (where), and warum (why) are used to ask questions. For example, Wo wohnst du? (pronounced: voh vohnst doo) – Where do you live?

These grammar points will help you form sentences correctly and understand how the German language works.

Review of Useful Phrases

Let's look at some useful phrases you have learned that will help you in everyday conversations:

- **Introducing Yourself:** Mein Name ist... (pronounced: mine nah-meh ist) – My name is...

- **Asking for Help:** Können Sie mir helfen? (pronounced: koe-nen zee meer hel-fen) – Can you help me?

- **Ordering Food:** Ich hätte gern... (pronounced: ikh he-teh gairn) – I would like...

- **Talking About Family:** Hast du Geschwister? (pronounced: hahst doo ge-shvist-er) – Do you have siblings?

These phrases will be very useful when you speak with German speakers in different settings.

FINAL REVIEW AND ASSESSMENT

Review of Cultural Tips

Understanding a country's culture is important when learning a language. Here are some cultural tips you have learned about Germany:

- **Punctuality:** Being on time is very important in Germany. Make sure to arrive on time for appointments or meetings.

- **Recycling:** Germans take recycling seriously. Pay attention to the different bins for paper, plastic, and glass.

- **Greetings:** It is polite to greet people with a handshake and say Guten Tag (Good day) when you meet them.

- **Politeness:** Using polite words like Bitte (please) and Danke (thank you) is very important.

Knowing these cultural tips will help you fit in and make a good impression when visiting or living in Germany.

Assessment Exercises

Now it's time to see how much you remember! Here are some exercises to test your knowledge:

Exercise 1: Translate the Sentences

Translate these sentences from English to German:

- I am learning German.
- Can you help me?
- Where is the train station?
- I would like a glass of water, please.

Check your translations with the phrases you have learned throughout the book.

Exercise 2: Match the Words

Match the German word with its English meaning:

- **die Katze** – a. the dog
- **der Hund** – b. the house
- **das Haus** – c. the cat
- **die Schule** – d. the school

Review the vocabulary section to check your answers.

Exercise 3: Fill in the Blanks

Fill in the blanks with the correct German word:

- _____ (Good morning), how are you?
- I am new here. My name is _____.
- _____ (Please), where is the supermarket?

Use what you've learned to complete these sentences.

Key Points to Remember

- **Review Key Vocabulary:** Remember the essential words like greetings, polite words, and numbers.
- **Understand Basic Grammar:** Review nouns, verb conjugation, and present tense to form correct sentences.
- **Practice Useful Phrases:** Use everyday phrases to help you communicate effectively.
- **Know Cultural Tips:** Remember important cultural points like being punctual and polite.
- **Test Your Knowledge:** Use exercises to assess your understanding and see where you need more practice.

Great job completing this book! Keep practicing and exploring the German language, and you'll continue to improve!